Temporary Gods and Arbitrary Arrangements

"What does a philosopher or poet fix?
Maybe the universe?"

~Angelo Letizia

Also by author:

Letizia, A.J. (2024). *Poetic Inquiry and arts-based research for the maintenance of the Republic and what comes after: A Vision for Metamodernity.* Routledge.

Letizia, A.J. (2024). *Learning to love in Winter.* Victoria, Australia: In Case of Emergency Press.

Letizia, A.J. (2024). *There is still beauty here.* British Columbia: Silver Bow Press.

Letizia, A.J. (2022). *Toward the real: Poems for a new reality.* Victoria, Australia: In Case of Emergency Press.

Letizia, A.J. (2022). *We are the winding down.* British Columbia: Silver Bow Press.

Letizia, A.J. (2022). *Pilgrims of infinity.* British Columbia: Silver Bow Press.

Letizia, A.J. (2021). *The starry devil and other unwanted poems.* British Columbia: Silver Bow Press.

Temporary Gods
and
Arbitrary Arrangements

by

Angelo Letizia

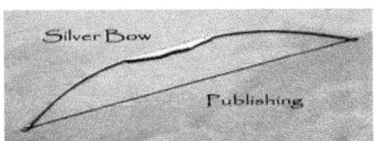

720 – Sixth Street, Unit # 5
New Westminster, BC
V3L 3C5   CANADA

Title: Temporary Gods and Arbitrary Arrangements"
Author: Angelo Letizia
Cover Art: "Moon Over Arctic Ice Waters" **painting by Candice James**
Layout and Design: Candice James
Editor: Candice James

All rights reserved including the right to reproduce or translate this book or any portions thereof, in any form without the permission of the publisher. Except for the use of short passages for review purposes, no part of this book may be reproduced, in part or in whole, or transmitted in any form or by any means, electronically or mechanically, also including photocopying, recording, or any information or storage retrieval system without prior permission in writing from the publisher or a licence from the Canadian Copyright Collective Agency (Access Copyright).

www.silverbowpublishing.com
info@silverbowpublishing.com
© Silver Bow Publishing 2025
ISBN: 9781774033494 book
ISBN: 9781774033500 e book

Library and Archives Canada Cataloguing in Publication

Title: Temporary gods and arbitrary arrangements / by Angelo Letitzia.
Names: Letizia, Angelo, author.
Identifiers: Canadiana (print) 20250145243 | Canadiana (ebook) 20250153165 | ISBN 9781774033494
 (softcover) | ISBN 9781774033500 (Kindle)
Subjects: LCGFT: Novels.
Classification: LCC PS3612.E79 T46 2025 | DDC 813/.6—dc23

Temporary Gods and Arbitrary Arrangements

*Huddled, in a cold room
Around a candle
Which does not emit
Much light
Hoping that
Despite being
Hungry and naked
We will be remembered
In some way, as
Resisting progress*

Temporary Gods and Arbitrary Arrangements

CONTENTS

Chapter   1 — year 2030 / 13
Chapter   2 — year 2027 / 21
Chapter   3 — year 2030 / 30
Chapter   4 — year 2014 / 40
Chapter   5 — year 2014 / 46
Chapter   6 — year 2015 / 51
Chapter   7 — year 2015 / 61
Chapter   8 — year 2025 / 65
Chapter   9 — year 2030 / 74
Chapter 10 — year 2025 / 79
Chapter 11 — year 2028 / 85
Chapter 12 — year 2023 / 89
Chapter 13 — year 2027 / 99
Chapter 14 — year 2027 / 103
Chapter 15 — year 2030 / 110
Chapter 16 — year 2030 / 115
Chapter 17 — year 2030 / 124
Chapter 18 — year 2030 / 135
Chapter 19 — year 2030 / 141
Chapter 20 — year 2032 / 145
Chapter 21 — year 2032 / 150
Chapter 22 — year 2032 / 159
Chapter 23 — year 2032 / 166
Chapter 24 — year 2032 / 172
Chapter 25 — year 2032 / 175
Chapter 26 — year 2032 / 185
Chapter 27 — year 2032 / 192
Author Profile / 200

Temporary Gods and Arbitrary Arrangements

Preface

I know you wanted a story. A nice, linear tale with a defined start and end. I know you wanted believable characters you could empathize with; and I know you wanted imagery that could make you see. And believe me, I tried. I really did. I tried to craft this type of story for you. But, instead, you got *this*. In the recesses of my brain, the idea of a "slice of life" is rolling around. I think I learned that in 8th grade. Maybe that is what this is, some slice of life vignette peppered with poetry and armchair philosophical insights. Each chapter does not lead neatly into the next, instead the chapters jerk around, bounding from one topic to the next. (Maybe it's like Ma Joad said, a man lives in jerks).

I am not skilled enough to create that smooth continuity. I am sorry. I know this is not what most people want. They do not want philosophy and poetry; they want witty characters and fun plots; they want Jesus and puppy dogs and fantasy or lighthearted mystery. This is why I no longer attend my writing group. I made them uncomfortable with my thoughts. But I cannot shed who I am. I do think there are insights here. I do think there are some empathetic characters, and there is something of a story. I know this book will not win any awards.

Maybe though, this is closer to real life. Real life is not a little story with a defined plot and neat story arc that wraps up after 200 pages or 2 hours on television. Real life does not follow a plot or conform to neat storylines like man versus nature or man versus technology (other things I learned in 8th grade). Real life is the present, but it's also memories and dreams. You don't win awards for living (maybe you should?). No, life, real lived life, is a series of stops and starts. It's a fight with your wife or attending your daughter's basketball game; it is a family member's illness. It is the sun that falls on a dilapidated farmhouse, or a rusted car in a field. Real life defies any confines we try to give it or any narrative we try to fit it into.

Introduction

One life in the middle of seven billion, a pulsating, living breathing thing outside of the confines of any logical system, blood, electricity, hearts, bones, and brains reeling, writhing, sleeping. A hierarchy of bones and gods. One life, or two lives or a family, an infinitesimal fraction of humanity, an unnoticed, uncared for speck in the infinite vast cold cosmos. What does it matter? What does one life matter, or two or three or a thousand? Millions die unnoticed, unloved, unwanted, neglected and forgotten. One small family floating like driftwood in the sea. One arbitrary configuration of atoms, cells, emotions and sinew. But there is life here, there is will, there is blood there is milk, life, and death. What does one family mean? One group or individual? What impact do they have on the universe? Do these individual lives of blood and thoughts and skin drive the human throng to commit murders, topple governments, lead revolutions and fall in love?

These events are transient fickle things though. Dreams and memories are the only glue of the universe, binding each life together. Each human dream is a new architecture, built in the cold cosmos among the primeval organisms and one celled tyrants, a celestial undertaking;

millions dream of these daily utopias and dystopias, cluttering the universe. The dying and the neglected, the forsaken and starving remember as well. They remember the sun in the fields of their youth. They remember their old lovers, dreams and memories and these are the only tangible things which drive the human throng forward, giving it goals and plans, the reason it trudges toward an uncertain future. Dreams and memories in the middle of their loneliness, like a rotted pumpkin in a large field, dreams and memories spring up, congeal and become a topography of blood, batteries of the universe, they are temporary, but this is progress, transient as it is.

Chapter 1
Year: 2030

The only noises in the room were the rhythmic beeping of the vital sounds monitor and the Darth Vader-esque breathing of the ventilator. The clock read 3:31 am. Joseph had heard somewhere that many enlightened people considered the time between two am and five am the "spiritual hours," because this is a time of stillness, quiet and peace, and it is during this time when many people have their great insights and ideas. But right now, he didn't have any great insights or ideas, he just had to pee because he drank too much coffee. He got up and used the restroom. When he finished he walked back over to the chair he had been sitting in. As he walked past his wife's bed, he noticed in the moonlight how some of her raggedy brown hair hung limply over her eyes. Obviously at this point it didn't matter, she couldn't see and would most likely never wake up. But instinctively, he brushed the hair away. He also noticed the top part of her breast poked out of the hospital gown. He gently moved the cloth over to cover it. He also couldn't help but smile as his fingers accidently rubbed against her breast.

Twenty years ago, this would have been sexy and exciting. Now it was just routine. After all this, though, she still had her looks. He remembered her as she used to be. Shapely and athletic, strong and independent. Fierce at times. Beautiful.

He'd had too much coffee and couldn't sleep. He must have drunk the whole goddamn pot. The shitty hospital coffee just went down like water. He examined all the complicated documents related to her care: the insurance bills, the impending funeral expenses. He just kept drinking the shitty coffee that burned his stomach. He never liked coffee and she did. Once he finally relented and tried it, he was hooked. They used to always drink coffee together. He didn't smoke regularly, but he sometimes used a cigar - just something to mindlessly puff on. He remembered seeing some "It's a Boy!" cigars in the gift shop and decided to pick some up when they opened. A little morbid, but he didn't care. He might start smoking a little more and drinking a little less coffee, trading once vice for another.

It had begun to snow outside, and he just watched, transfixed. It didn't snow much anymore, like when he was a kid. So, whenever it did snow, he always made a point to watch. By tomorrow it would probably turn to rain and the streets would be a fucking mess with gravel and trash. But right now, he just enjoyed the solemnity of it all. There had always been a peacefulness to the snow.

He remembered when he was in school, 8th grade maybe, reading a Jack London story about a man and a dog who were traversing some snow-covered tundra. The dog died, and the man had used all his matches so could not make a fire, and he froze to death.

But the way London described this death, the succumbing to nature, to the barren white snow, always stuck with Joseph. Even in 8th grade. He was never a great student, always just okay, and he probably did shitty on the test, but that story always stuck with him. He envisioned the endless white snow in the moon light and a lonely man dying, accepting his fate. A solitary man, peacefully dying in the welcoming snow. And it was beautiful. He always thought of that story whenever it snowed.

From the fifth floor he could see an ambulance hurriedly pull in to the hospital. The driver and passenger quickly flung their doors open and then opened the back door. Even from up here, he could hear frantic voices, although he could not make out what they were saying. A nurse fitted what looked to be a man with some type of tube. He watched as the nurses and paramedics wheeled the person into the entrance way and the nurses disappeared. The ambulance stayed a few minutes longer while the driver filled out a paper and then drove away. He could not see the person well but he did see a blood-spattered sheet. The ambulance left faint tire marks in the newly fallen snow. Hopefully, this person had a better fate then the protagonist in London's story.

He rummaged through his bag and found a warm apple which he instantly devoured. The sweet juice dribbled down his face and soaked his goatee. He chomped the apple to the core and then threw it away in the wastebasket which was about three feet from his wife's bed. As he carelessly threw out the core, it clumsily knocked over the whole can, and garbage spilled out everywhere as the soft plastic of the wastebasket itself thumped on the floor. Food wrappers, Q-tips, bandages and now an apple core were strewn on the linoleum, in a weird sort of impromptu mosaic.

"Fuck." He sighed and shook his head as he cleaned up the mess.

Just then, the ventilator made a strange, high-pitched screech. He froze with the apple core in his hand and stared at his wife. *"Was this it?"* He squeezed the core and sugary juice greased his hands, he squeezed so hard the core collapsed and he held two smaller pieces, crumbled up.

Finally, the machine resumed its normal tone. Joseph dropped the core on the ground and walked over to inspect the monitors. Heart rate and breathing were normal. Everything seemed fine again. He collected himself and went back to picking up the trash. His hand was sticky from the smashed apple juice so he went to the restroom to wash it off.

"Jesus" he said out loud to no one. He had been preparing for his wife's death. In fact, in some way he wanted it to come. He just wanted this to be over with. But when he suddenly faced that prospect it scared the shit out of him.

Over the last ten years his wife had steadily deteriorated. Little by little, and then rapidly, her illness forced him into a caregiving role. As the children got older, they were able to help with tasks like driving and cooking. His wife had stopped driving, then stopped cooking and cleaning. Before they had moved her to an assisted living facility, she could barely get off the couch. The MS. had ravaged her mind and body.

Whenever anyone talked to her, she increasingly had a deer-in-headlights look. Joseph did not know how much she comprehended toward the end. Once she fell into a coma, he just wanted it to be over.

One thought that continually cropped up in his head, was the thought of his wife with her previous lovers. And he couldn't help but thinking all of her former lovers were together, laughing at him somewhere in the universe, laughing at him for being stuck with her. Why did he think this? He never told anyone of that thought, but it was always there, like a cancer.

Caregiving definitely required patience, something he sorely lacked. Like Vicky always pointed out, he resembled his mother, quick to anger, irritable and always ready to fly off the handle at the slightest inconvenience. These qualities had made him a less-than-optimal caregiver.

His impatience with her grew. He would become visibly annoyed when she walked slowly with her cane. He complained when he had to push her around in the wheelchair or load the goddamn scooter which weighed over a 100 pounds. It used to send him into a rage when the house was filthy and she slept on the couch. He resented her, and sometimes, he downright hated her.

"Hello?" A nurse popped her head into the door, interrupting his thoughts.

"Hi." Joseph said, a little startled.

"I saw the monitor started beeping and wanted to come in." The nurse said.

"Yea, it scared me. But she seems to be okay now."

The nurse inspected the monitor. "Yes, she is okay; it really isn't anything to worry about.

It seems like it was a slight fluctuation in her electrical signals. This happens from time to time."

"Thank you for coming in." He said wearily to the nurse.

"Are you getting any sleep?" she asked with a concerned smile.

"A little...not really." He said.

"All of that is normal. Unfortunately, I've seen many people in your shoes. The hospital can recommend counselors if you need one."

"Thank you," Joseph lied. "Maybe I will." Vicky had been on him to see a counselor for a long time. He had gone, early in their marriage, but he never found it really helpful. Some random nurse had also encouraged him to go to counselling at the end of his marriage as well.

The nurse smiled and left the room.

He finally felt somewhat tired. Maybe the monitor scare exhausted him. He attempted to sleep again. He found the hospital furniture surprisingly comfortable. He took the blanket and pillow and rested. There were little metal studs in the fake leather chair and the moon caught them in such a way that they glowed an eerie white, like little communion tables lining the underside of the chair. The rhythmic beeping now soothed him.

He almost fell asleep when something caught his eye on the floor; the apple core. He thought he had cleaned it up but the top half of the apple rested at the foot of his wife's hospital bed. Even in the moonlight, he could see it had already turned a sickly brown. He fell asleep without picking it up.

Chapter 2
Year: 2027

Vicky opened the pantry door to retrieve the broom and dust pan. This used to be a simple job. She wobbled on her feet but steadied herself long enough to position the dustpan on the floor then leaned on the broom. She began to sweep the kitchen floor in choppy strokes, most of the dust and debris missing the dustpan and scattering behind the hutch with the China plates.

"Dammit." She muttered to herself.

She continued to sweep, but one of her sweeping strokes was too long and it took her off balance. She tried to use the broom again to steady herself, but the bristles slipped out on the slick linoleum floor. She grasped for the hutch but her fingers only grazed the wood. She fell hard on her bottom. The broom flung itself across the kitchen and she kicked the dust pan on the fall down. What little dust was in there created a small cloud before dissipating.

"Fuck!" she yelled out to no one.

Joseph would be angry with her if he knew she attempted housework. Of course, he would probably still complain about the messy house, so she could not win.

She began to assess the damage. Nothing seemed broken or sprained. She did not hit her head. Her butt ached and there would probably be a bruise, but she fell on the fleshy, meaty part. Instead of standing up, she crawled on her knees to collect the dustpan and broom. She shoved them both in the pantry, but there was too much shit in pantry and the broom fell on top of her. She shoved it in again, but it fell again.

"Goddamn it!"

She shoved the broom as hard as she could and slammed the pantry door all while sitting on her bottom. As she shoved the door closed she winced with pain. She heard the broom knock into the closed door and she began to cry, glad no one was home to hear her.

This used to be so easy and now she couldn't even sweep the fucking floor.

Like an aging jalopy, rusted out, belts spinning and breaking, bald tires. But no, actually, she is only 45 and was diagnosed when 33. She is young and should not be breaking down. But there is no logic here. Logic dies in the rain. There is only her broken form, a rusted-out skeleton of what she used to be. And there was no cause, no reason, just blind chance. The universe is a lottery of pain and suffering.

In moments of anger, Joseph would accuse her of not taking care of herself, she drank too much in college or she fucked too many guys, or she didn't eat right. These comments were incredibly hurtful, and they would fight over them, but deep down she knew Joseph just lashed out, and looked for someone, something to blame and could find no one and nothing. There are no causes just effects in this lonely universe.

She crawled over to the couch and fell asleep. She didn't care if the floor was dirty.

***

"How was work today?"

"Boring, as usual. We had to sit through hours worth of useless trainings and presentations."

"Same people talk?" Vicky asked.

"Same goddam people ask the same stupid questions. We hear the same stupid shit every year. I just did work on my laptop. How was your day?" Joseph asked.

"I fell again." She said bluntly.

"Bad?"

"Not too bad, I don't think. I fell on my butt." She said sheepishly.

"Does it hurt?" he asked.

"A little."

"Do you want me to check it?" he said with a grin, half serious.

"Actually, yea. Can you see if I have bruise?"

"A free look at your butt?" Of course!"

They both walked up the stairs. Vicky moved slowly and Joseph walked behind her. In the bathroom Vicky steadied herself by the counter by putting her hands on it. Joseph wiggled her pants down and knelt besides her; she stood, shivering, in her underwear.

"Ready?" he asked?

"Do it." She said.

He pulled down her underwear- the blue ones with the frayed elastic band – down to her knees.

"See anything?" She cocked her head back to try and see him.

He gently prodded her butt to inspect it.

"Yea, there is a pretty nasty red mark here." He circled the area lightly with his finger.

"Yea that is exactly where I fell. It hurts."

"I think I need to inspect it more..." he said mischievously.

"Okay, I think you looked long enough. If you stay down there, I might fart." She said jokingly with a smile.

"Hmmm" he drew this out, smiled and licked his lips.
"Just help me get my pants on you pig."

He laughed as he pulled up her underwear and helped her back into her pants. She struggled down the stairs and they both sat on the couch. Inspecting her butt or other parts of her body for bruises had become commonplace; it almost made both of them forget her loss of dignity. Vicky an aging star, burning out, turning to ice, a cold rock which would drift until pulled by some gravitational force.

"Mid-day Coffee?" he asked.

"Yes please. Just be sure to wash your hands first." She smirked.

"Got it." He washed his hands and began to make coffee.

Vicky pulled her sweatshirt cord around the hood a little tighter to block the cold.
They sat on the couch.

"They didn't even put out coffee for us today. I didn't expect a 7-course lunch, but at least some coffee." Joseph sipped silently.

"Yea, that's crazy. How much could it cost to make a big pot of coffee?"
At that moment, the door opened.

"Hey, how was school?" Vicky asked Rita. Rita barely acknowledged them as she put her bookbag down next to the door (something Vicky had specifically asked her not to do).

"Fine." She said, heading to her room.

Vicky and Joseph shot each other a look. "She seems to be in a lovely mood." Joseph whispered.

"And of course, she didn't move her bag. But I am not saying anything, not with her in a mood like that."

"Agreed." Joseph said. They both sipped their coffee silently.

***

"This is really good. Who made this?" Ron asked as he scooped himself another helping of pasta and sauce.

"Dad and I." Rita said.

"Well, mostly her." Joseph nudged Rita. "What do you call me, the sous chef?"

Rita smiled. "Yea, I learned that term from Ratatouille, its like a helper chef."

"I'm okay with that." Joseph smiled. "I boiled water for the pasta and put in the bread to bake, she did the hard work, making the sauce."

"It all tastes great." Vicky smiled, So, how was everyone's day at school?"Sometimes it was difficult to get teenagers to talk. Bridgette went first. When she finished, Vicky asked the two older ones.

"Uh, okay." Said Ron. "Got an A on my GIS quiz."

"Nice," said Vicky.

"I finally finished my physics packet and got an A. That class is killing me." Rita said.

"Well, whatever you do, it will be better than me." Joseph said to her. "Physics is the only class I ever failed in high school."

"You failed it?" Rita asked.

"Yes, I just didn't care, thought I could skate by like I skated by in every class. That didn't work in physics." He took a forkful of pasta. A little bit of sauce dribbled into his goatee and he quickly wiped it up.

Vicky stood up and wobbled. She took two unsteady steps before stopping to collect herself.

"Mom, what are you doing?" Rita asked.

"Just getting some water." Vicky replied, a little annoyed.

"Sit down. Let me get it." Vicky went back to her seat and Rita filled up a cup of water and placed it in front of Vicky.

"We don't need another fall." Joseph said.

Chapter 3
Year: 2030

The room lightened up despite the clouds outside. And cold. The clock read 7:32 am. He had finally dozed off for a few hours. Vicky lay in the bed, unmoved from the night before. The beeping filled the room. And now he needed food. He checked himself in the bathroom mirror. He didn't look too bad, but he felt like he might smell a little. He rummaged through his bag and found some cologne and deodorant. He threw some water on his face and walked down to the cafeteria.

"Excuse me." A pleasant looking blond woman in her thirties interrupted him.

He looked up. "Can I have this chair?" she asked. "Of course," he said with a smile. She carried the chair back to her table where a good-looking young guy sat with her. He watched them for a moment. They sipped coffee and laughed. They were probably in their late twenties.

Joseph dug into his bag, opened his laptop, and turned it on. The password box for the learning management system his college used flashed on the screen and he entered his password. His grade book popped up. Seventeen new notifications- seventeen new final essays. His wife may be dying, but he still had to work and pay the bills. He opened the first essay from his student Kathryn Jones. He had never met any of these students, most he had not even seen. Sometimes they might have a little picture associated with their name.

At that moment he noticed an aging woman who hobbled into the cafeteria with a walker. Next to her stood a hospital orderly. His mother called it "people watching." The woman trudged to the food line. She pointed to the orderly and indicated what food she wanted and the orderly, with a disinterested look on his face, collected her food and they both proceeded to the register.

Kathryn Jones had chosen the Hegel Schopenhauer prompt for her final essay. The prompt read:

Which philosopher, Georg Wilhelm Friedrich Hegel or Arthur Schopenhauer, more accurately described the emerging modern world of early 19th century? Create a thesis statement which outlines your argument and support your answer with examples from the thinkers. In addition, place all ideas in historical context.

Joseph mused on the prompt he had written for his students. For Hegel, and his followers, writing in the early 19th century, all historical events, from the Fall of the Roman Empire to the Storming of the Bastille, were part of a larger design. Not the design of some otherworldly being, not a god in the sky with a white beard, no, these events were part of what Hegel called the "world spirit," something akin to reason. It was the product of all of humanity through all time. In fact, Hegel had believed that humanity, in his day, had reached, what he called, triumphantly, "the end of history," the pinnacle of existence, and he believed it would only get better.

The sounds of clanking silverware and inaudible voices crisscrossed the half full cafeteria. The familiar cafeteria smell of fried foods, specifically meat and potatoes, wafted to him. Bacon sizzled somewhere in the kitchen. In the far corner of the room he saw a middle-aged woman eating what seemed to be a bowl of cereal.

As a young child, he used to watch people for hours. He would make up stories about them. This woman was a secret agent, this man was an actor, this person was a professional athlete, etcetera. Now, he just appreciated the different people he saw. He still wondered about their lives though. He especially liked to observe people sitting alone. Some looked sad, some looked weary, others looked content, like they knew some sort of secret. He wondered what he looked like to an observer.

Hegel's philosophy gripped continental Europe for a few decades. By the latter part of the 19th century however, the ideas of another philosopher, Arthur Schopenhauer were much more in vogue. Schopenhauer did not see any goals, or reason or progress. No, he only saw what he called "the will," something Freud would take up later on. While humans may seem like rational creatures, they, and all of existence, were driven by will, irrational desire, which used reason to obtain its ends. Our vaunted reason is only a puppet, the strings of which are pulled by raw, visceral will, and this only serves to help us kill each other more efficiently. And almost on cue, as Joseph thought this to himself, he happened to glance to the television which blared out the news which almost always seemed to confirm Schopenhauer's ideas.

"Excuse me." A gruff looking man half-heartedly apologized for knocking into him as he balanced a tray of breakfast food and walked to a table a few feet away from Joseph.

"No worries." Joseph muttered back, he did not think the man could hear him anymore though.

Schopenhauer saw no meaning to existence, no end-point, no grand ethical system, no absolute reason, no god. No, he only saw nihilism and irrationality, purposelessness.

Kathryn's paper contained a highly detailed and original thesis. She then proceeded to supply examples from the philosophers to construct her case. She had argued that while Hegel might be more comforting, she believed that Schopenhauer more accurately described the emerging modern world. She noted that Schopenhauer died in 1860 and did not live to see the rise of some of the most horrible episodes in human history, such as the negative effects of industrialization, the slums, the factories and the robber barons, the World Wars, mass genocides, nuclear weapons and all the rest. She did not believe in progress. He gave the paper an "A".

Jessica Caton, another student in his class, wrote the next paper. She argued that Hegel had made the better argument. While there was a tremendous amount of suffering, wars, famine and poverty, both in the 19th century and even today, Jessica pointed to the truly amazing progress that had been made with regards to Civil Rights, medicine, technology and transportation, just to name a few areas. She had supplied excellent examples. An "A" paper.

But something else had struck Joseph in Jessica's paper, her treatment of technology. She pointed out that we, as a species, may be nearing the point of "singularity," or the instant where humanity and technology merge. Today our cell phones were outside of us, in a few years they might literally be part of us, along with electronic pacemakers and microchips. Jessica used the notion of singularity as a Hegelian indicator of progress. In a bold move, Jessica argued the end of history, human history, might be the singularity. Wow.

Joseph reread her paper. There was a sort of exhilaration when a student surpassed him- he loved it. He never felt any twinge of jealously. This was an incredible argument. Not one he could totally agree with, but an excellent argument, nonetheless. He glanced back at Kathryn's papers and reread a passage she had written.

Progress is illusionary, something we comfort ourselves with. Specifically, our technological progress. Technology only allows us to kill more efficiently. At this point in human history, we could feed, clothe and house every individual on this planet. No one needs to suffer. But what do we do? We still kill each other, cheat each other, rape each other, make profit at each other's expense and then we pray and preach and tell each other how moral we are. Schopenhauer foresaw this, accurately described what we are. There is no goal or salvation, no god or machine will save us. The only "end" is annihilation and/or planetary destruction.

Two world views crashed together with no resolution, beyond even what their authors had anticipated. And even the lives of Hegel and Schopenhauer bear out their competing philosophies in some ways.

Joseph always pointed out to his class that Schopenhauer was truly an asshole and a bit of a womanizer. Perhaps Schopenhauer embodied his own view of humanity, and his own ideas of purposelessness and immorality. Schopenhauer once pushed an old woman down a flight of stairs after they had an argument in his apartment complex. The court ordered him to pay the old woman until her death. When she finally did die, Schopenhauer supposedly declared: "I am glad that bitch is dead." Schopenhauer knew of Hegel, they were contemporaries. He hated him, despised him and scheduled his lectures at the same time as Hegel at the university of Berlin. No one came to Schopenhauer's lectures and instead opted for the more popular Hegel. Schopenhauer quit academia and lived off his father's inheritance for the rest of his life. By the later 19th century, Hegel and his progress were almost forgotten. The only progress was a Darwinian progress, a survival of the fittest, which Schopenhauer in many ways presaged.

Joseph checked his email.

Dear Dr. Joy
Thank you for your submission to our journal. Unfortunately, your submission does not fit our needs at this time.

Not a surprise.

He shook his head to himself, to nobody. That article he had submitted centered on Hegel and Schopenhauer and the idea of historical progress, but as he slowly realized no one cared about this topic, or maybe, he just wasn't a good enough writer. Either way, he stared at the rejection notice, which had become all too common for him in his career.

He also knew why Kathryn had picked that argument. While he had never met Kathryn in person, he did have a zoom call with her once. Her grades had dropped and she requested to meet. He found out that she had just gotten out of a severely abusive relationship with her boyfriend, and as a result also had financial trouble. After some time, she had gotten back on her feet, but he could only imagine what that had done to her. Was there progress for her?

He thought of his wife in the bed upstairs. He thought of Kathryn, and then he thought larger and pictured Nazi concentration camps, the Stalinist purges, pollution, industrial slums, demagogic politicians, child hunger. He could not say definitively if he sided with Hegel, but sometimes, it proved difficult to argue with

Schopenhauer. Another memory instantly struck him.

One summer day, a few years ago, he was outside playing with his youngest daughter. He came inside with his daughter to get a drink and cool off. As he opened the back door, Vicky sat on the kitchen floor, eating a tapioca pudding out of cup with a children's spoon because they were easier for her to handle. He looked down at her, eating this pudding. She was fucking pathetic. There were deep lines on her face and a bruise on her bare foot from when she fell last. He thought of Kathryn, her black eye still fresh when he met with her on zoom. Is this progress? Is this where the world spirit leads? To a disabled woman eating pudding on a dirty linoleum floor? Is this the goal? Maybe this is the end of history. What a fucking joke.

Joseph suddenly remembered what the poet Ezra Pound had once said. Humanity thinks itself intelligent but chews on pig's ass. Joseph looked over to the good-looking couple. The man ate what looked like a bacon, egg and cheese sandwich. Joseph could only smile to himself. He sat alone and knew the secret.

Chapter 4
Year: 2014

Vicky lay exhaustedly, but peacefully, asleep in the hospital bed. Bridgette also lay peacefully asleep in the little hospital gurney next to her having only been born a few hours ago. Ronald, their seven-year-old, played with Lego's on the floor, and five-year-old Rita played on the other side of the room with her My Little Ponies. Both the ponies and the Legos were gifts from Bridgette, or so Ronald and Rita were told. Both understood this was a ruse, but a playful one, and both were happy to get new toys. Joseph went back and forth between Ronald and Rita, playing Legos and ponies.

"Daddy." Rita whispered. "Play ponies with me." She motioned him over with her hand.

"Okay," he whispered back

Their family governing unit, while young, began to take its final shape, as it was understood that Bridgette would be the final child. But Vicky emerged as the living beating heart of that unit. There were no hard feelings over this situation either. Joseph never wanted to be a tyrant like most of the men in his family. He wanted what was best for the children, and two equal parents seemed best.

"Daddy, I am going to line up all of these ponies here. They are going to celebrate."

Joseph supposed all families had a governing structure, but they were unstable, fickle and temporary configurations.

"Daddy, you be the pink pony." Rita handed Joseph a pink sparkly pony while she held onto a translucent orange pony with a picture of a soda can on the hind legs.

"Okay," Joseph said with a smile. "What should I do?" He asked his daughter. She had a focused look on her five-year-old face.

"You make the pony drink from the pond. I am going to feed this pony apples. And then they will go to a party together." There were no other props or toys, Rita imagined all of this in her head and Joseph played along. He had set out a blanket on the hospital floor for her to lay on, even though the floor was surprisingly clean. Rita than took a sip of water from her cup and ate a few animal crackers before resuming her horse tending.

Joseph, against his wishes, gradually became the sole leader of his family. At first the MS did not impact their lives, but it quickly began to rob Vicky of most of her normal functioning. He slowly became the tyrant he despised.

"Dad. Let's set up a fighting ring with these guys." Ron handed a Lego mini-figure to Joseph.

"Okay." Joseph said. He began to arrange the Legos into a ring.

"Who should I be?" Joseph asked his son. Ever serious, Ron thought hard about it before handing him a blue mini-figure."

"You take this one dad. His name is Kai."

"I know who Kai is." Joseph smiled and began to play Legos with his son on the floor.

"Just making sure dad."

After a few minutes, he went to check on Bridgette. "Gimme a sec bud." He said to Ron.

He walked over to the gurney. His daughter lay peacefully. He watched her face, still puffy with birth, move slightly as she breathed. He put his ear to her face and heard little breaths. Her pink hat was pulled just to her eye line and a blanket was pulled up to her chin. A new arrangement.

***

"Hey." Vicky meekly said.

"Oh, hey." Joseph was started. "I didn't know you were awake"

"Did Kelly take Ron and Rita home?"

"Yes, about an hour ago." Joseph said.

"Good. How did they seem?"

"They seemed okay. Happy with their new toys." Joseph smiled.

"I bet." Vicky said. "Is the nursery all ready for Bridgette?"

"Almost." Joseph smiled.

"It's not done?" Vicky frowned.

"It's almost done. I just have to assemble the bookshelf."

"Make sure it is done by Wednesday when we come home." She said, a little sternly.

"I will, I will. I just need to put the finishing touches on my dissertation."

Vicky frowned slightly but did not say anything.

"Did they miss much school?" Vicky asked.

"Not really. Ron missed a half day."

"Make sure you work with him to get any missed work in."

"I will." Joseph said.

"When I come home, I want to have some time with each kid. One day, I want to take Ron to the zoo or something, and then I want to take Rita somewhere too." Vicky shifted herself in the bed which in her condition was a major undertaking.

"Okay," Joseph laughed "But recover first."

"It's important they don't feel neglected or unloved."

"I know." Joseph said.

Bridgette stirred in her little gurney and began to cry.

"Oh, I think it's time for her feeding." Vicky said. "Can you hand her to me?"

Joseph nodded and went over to the gurney. He gently scooped up baby Bridgette. She weighed 8 pounds, 4 ounces. Joseph cradled her in his arms. She began to cry and he handed her to Vicky who nestled her in the crook of her arm and began to nurse her. Bridgette quieted down.

Chapter 5
Year: 2014

"Congratulations *Doctor* Joy!"

Joseph's dissertation advisor welcomed him back into the room after his committee deliberated.

Joseph did not say anything for a moment, he just basked in the moment. He had done it.

"You did a great job on the defense." His advisor said. The other members of Joseph's committee also congratulated him.

"Anyone want to go out for beers?" Joseph asked.

A group of people went to a local bar, including Joseph, his advisors and some of

Joseph's classmates who had not defended their dissertations yet.

The waitress set down Joseph's order. He took a sip of his drink.

"Well now," his advisor said. "Welcome to the community of scholars."

"It seems so surreal."

"What are your plans now?" One of his classmates asked him.

"I want to be a faculty member." Joseph said quickly. "Really, I want to do research and work at a larger research institution.

"And you can," his advisor said.

This had been his dream for years. Work at a prestigious institution and build a research profile.

"Do you have applications out?" Another classmate asked him.

"Yes some, but I was waiting until I defended."

"Are you going to pursue your dissertation topic as your research agenda?"

"I think so."

"That might change or at least look a little different. Either way it is a good topic to pursue." his advisor said.

"I think I want to pursue the line of citizenship and political formations that I worked out in my dissertation."

"I think it's a good line of research." His advisor said. "Keep building on it. Keep fleshing out what citizenship looks like in this volatile political time."

"My only concern..." Joseph said in-between sips of diet soda and mouthfuls of steak "...is, will this line of research be attractive to research universities?"

"That is the question." His advisor said. "You just don't know. In some ways, this entire system is broken. Sometimes, niche research like yours gets overlooked because the large research universities only care about certain types of research."

"Yea, I sensed that." Joseph said.

Another student spoke up. "So, if you do research in an area that a larger prestigious university doesn't care for, then you get overlooked?"

Joseph's advisor spoke. "Not always, but a lot of times yes."

Another student spoke up. "I also heard they really only value research articles and do not care for books or essays."

Joseph's advisor spoke up once more "Again, there is some truth in that. Generally, getting published in the prestigious journals will boost your profile considerably. And like big universities, journals cater to specific ideas."

"Sounds rigged." Another student said.

"I wouldn't say its rigged, but there are incentives to pursue certain types of research." Joseph's advisor said. She paused a moment. "I would also say this entire system structures what success looks like and in some ways, can stifle creativity and innovative scholarship."

A waiter came and refilled some drinks.

"But I don't want to discourage anyone to pursue what they want. Just know there are certain advantages to pursue certain topics. And, I would add that sometimes certain research makes itself known and people recognize it. A skilled researcher can carve out a nice place for him or herself."

Joseph was silent for a while. With his PhD he was one step closer to achieving his goal. He believed he had important ideas and they needed to be shared. He wanted to help humanity in some small way, light a path forward, but, like anything, there would be obstacles. He did not know if the big universities or the prestigious research journals would be keen on his research.

Chapter 6
Year: 2015

"What did they say?" Joseph asked as he poured noodles into the boiling water which screamed, bubbled, and hissed.

"They think ,,, it's probably MS."

"Really? Holy shit." Was all he could muster.

"Yeah, since he'is only the general practitioner, he said he can't give me an official diagnosis. I will have to go to a neurologist."

"So, what does that mean?" Joseph asked.

Vicky put down her purse and put her shoes in corner. She hung up her car keys.

"Well, first, I have to make an appointment with the neurologist. But I think we mostly just monitor it. The GP said most people can live something close to a normal life with MS. Something like 85% cases are pretty mild. Hopefully, I am one of those."

"Yea I hope so. I mean, right now, it seems it just makes you a little more tired. Hopefully, that's it."

"Yea. No one dies from MS." she said reassuringly. "Some peoples bodies break down and they contract other illnesses."

"Let's not talk about that." Joseph poured sauce over the pasta and added the meatballs. Vicky took the loaf of garlic bread out of the oven. She then picked up baby Bridgette and fastened her in the high chair. Ron and Rita took their places at the table and the family began to eat.

"Okay, everyone tell me about your day!" Vicky said. "Ron, you start." Vicky fed a spoonful of baby oatmeal to Bridgette. The oatmeal dribbled down her plump cheeks.

Temporary Gods and Arbitrary Arrangements

"I got the best helper award today!" Ron said enthusiastically. Mr. Winter said I was the best helper in all of second grade.

Vicky smiled. "Of course, you were! You are such an amazing boy." She then turned to Rita. "What about you Rita?"

"I painted a picture!" She said with glee. And then she showed it to everyone at the table.

"Beautiful!" Vicky said. "Daddy, look at Rita's picture." She gestured to Joseph.

"I love it." Joseph said to his daughter.

"What should we do after dinner?" Vicky wiped the oatmeal dribble from Bridgette's face.

"Let's play Candyland!" Rita said.

"Uno!" Ron said.

"Or..." Vicky smiled. "I was thinking we could do some crafts." She pulled out a box with supplies in it " Let's do potato crafts!"

"Potato crafts? What is that Mommy!" asked Rita.

"I guess you'll have to wait and see!" she smiled at her. "But you have to eat all your vegetables to find out."

Rita made a disgusted face. "I *hate* vegetables but I'll eat them so I can do potato crafts!"

"Don't say hate." Vicky gently reminded her daughter.

"Sorry Mommy."

"I want to do them to!" Ron said as he excitedly ate all of his broccoli.

"Daddy, do you want to do them?" Rita asked.

"Well, I have to work on my big paper for class." Joseph told her.

"You are always writing papers." She frowned.

"I know, but Daddy is trying to do something good! I want to help people with my writing. I want to help teachers and politicians. Maybe some day they will read it and it will help them." Joseph said confidently.

He thought he detected a subtle smirk from Vicky but did not pursue it.

"Okay Daddy." We'll make the potatoes without you. "Go write." She furrowed her brows.

***

"When you're applying for jobs, make sure to ask about the health insurance." Vicky said as she combed her hair.

"I will. I never really paid attention to that stuff but I guess we need to start." Joseph said as he put his book down and sat up in bed.

"Like we said before, hopefully, my MS doesn't get that bad. Have you applied to any jobs recently?" she asked him.

"A few opened up that look good for me. University of North Dakota, University of Cincinnati and University of Ohio. The postings are somewhat in line with my research."

"What are they asking for?"

"Cincinnati wants someone with a philosophical background, and North Dakota wants something similar."

"I thought you were not straight philosophy." Vicky asked as she laid down her brush.

"I'm not. My work doesn't really fit a type of genre, but I am hoping its close enough. Pam thinks I have a chance at a prestigious research university."

"She's been awesome to you." Vicky said.

"Yea she's an amazing dissertation chair."

Make sure you have her as a reference!" Vicky said as she made her eyes big. She walked over to the bed, took off her sweatshirt, and fastened the covers over herself. Joseph readjusted the covers after she tussled them.

"So annoying!" He playfully said to her. Vicky yanked the covers hard and Joseph was laying there with only the sheet half on.

"Jerk," he said. At that he pounced on top of her and began to kiss her.

"Make sure the door is closed!" She whispered loudly.

***

He and Vicky lay in bed, in the dark, exhausted after sex, but too wired to sleep.

"I guess my parents told my aunt about your PhD. Judy said to say congratulations."

"They told her?" he said bemused.

"Yea why is that surprising?" she asked a little incredulously.

"I just didn't think they cared enough to tell anyone. Your parents are not the biggest fans of education."

"Of course they care. It is a big achievement."

"Well, my parents certainly didn't care. And I don't believe yours do either. I think your uncle called me an 'educated idiot" one time."

"Stop. He didn't call you that, he just said it more generally."

"Either way, it was directed at me. But I am not singling out your family. My family does the same shit. My father constantly makes fun of educated people to my face."

"They just don't know any better. They were not raised with the drive to go to college and they work with their hands."

"I know, and there is nothing wrong with that. My dad is an amazing mechanic, your stepfather is an awesome handyman and I can't really do any of that shit. But it would be nice if they pretended to care or at least not insult me."

"I think you're too sensitive sometimes." Vicky turned to look at him in the dark.

"Yea, probably. But I think their attitudes are a larger symptom of the anti-intellectualism in this country."

"They are probably intimidated by you."

"But its not like I use big words or go out of my way to insult them or make them feel dumb. In fact, they do that to me with all the handyman shit." He could tell his voice was becoming more irritated.

"Even so, they probably feel inferior because you are so educated."

"The funny thing is I actually feel *less intelligent* now."

"What do you mean?" He could see Vicky had a curious look, the moonlight refracted on her face.

"Its like Socrates. The more I learn, I just keep realizing how ignorant I am."

And that was true, the more knowledge he had, the more he realized how much he didn't know.

"What time is it?" she asked. He checked the clock she couldn't see because her view was obstructed by a huge box of diapers.

"Almost midnight." He said.

"Think you can go one more round?" she smiled and put her hand on his chest.

His eyes opened wide. "Wow, horny tonight?"
He shifted and raised himself up on an elbow

Vicky began to kiss him.

"Actually, I think I am done tonight." She said quickly.

Temporary Gods and Arbitrary Arrangements

"Okay, okay..." he said with a smile

He closed his eyes and drifted off to sleep with his arm securely around her waist.

Chapter 7
Year: 2015

Hello Dr. Joy, it is nice to meet you in person. The women extended her hand, Joseph shook it firmly, but not too firmly.

"We have coffee, would you like some?" She asked Joseph.

"Ah, only if it is made."

"Of course! How do you take it?"

"Just black is fine."

"Really?" Deborah said to him as she scrunched her face. "I like mine loaded up with cream and sugar."

Both he and Deborah sat down at the table.

"Okay, so tell me about your research agenda." Deborah sipped her coffee and handed Joseph his cup.

"Dr. Worley..."

"Please, Deb." She put her hand up.

Joseph smiled and felt a little more at ease. "Likewise, call me Joe."

Deb smiled at him and waited for him to proceed. This was it. He had been preparing for this moment, well, really for years. At the start of his master's degree, he realized he did not want to teach high school anymore. As he worked through his master's and then his doctorate, the goal came more clearly into focus. He wanted to be a professor of education and he wanted to pursue a unique research agenda. He believed he had important things to say, and if given the chance, he believed people would listen.

"Well, my agenda, I think, touches on some unique and interesting ideas. For one, I study and publish on the notion of historical progress and what that means and if there really is progress. I have examined the notion of historical progress, as linked to education and its conjunction with the arts..." As Joseph continued to talk he kept looking at Deb's face to gauge her reaction. The warmness when she offered him a cup of coffee seemed to have dissipated, replaced with a mild look of concern. When he paused she spoke up.

"Where have you published?"

He was waiting for that question. He had just gotten word that one of his articles had been accepted by a prestigious journal. The article was not a full article, but a short theoretical exploration, but that shouldn't matter. He triumphantly told her the journal and she seemed impressed. Then he added "My article was in the Research in Brief Section."

The impressed look instantly faded. "That wouldn't count here." She said flatly. It has to be a full-length article.

"Oh," he said stupidly. He then rattled off some of his other publications and the book he was working on, but Deb did not really acknowledge these. When he finished talking, Deb noted that this sounded good, but she spoke unenthusiastically. He just lost the job.

"Okay, its time for lunch." She said.

They walked to the cafeteria and made small talk. He tried to hide his devastation. He truly believed that article would be his ticket to a professorship.

Chapter 8
Year: 2025

"Didn't I tell you about the wedding?" Joseph's father asked in a thick New York City accent.

"Yea, but I thought we had it worked out." Joseph said as he stood awkwardly by the chocolate covered pretzels.

"Oh." Lawrence said sheepishly. They had discussed this already. Joseph suspected his father just didn't want to fight his stepmother over Joseph and the family visiting.

"I am in a store, I can't talk right now." Joseph said flatly.

"Okay call me back." Lawrence said.

"Okay Bye." Joseph hung up the phone.

"What did he say?" Vicky asked when they got back into the car.

"Basically lied. I don't think he wanted to fight Ann Marie. She really didn't want us there after he invited us." Joseph said.

More family governance. Joseph's father was no dictator or tyrant. He was more like an absentee landlord, if anything.

"So, we are not going to New York for Christmas?" Vicky asked.

"I am not going there. I don't want to see them." Joseph said.

Rita looked on from the back, disappointed.

"I am sorry babe," he said to Rita. "I know you wanted to go to the city."

"Yea," she said dejectedly.

"But we can't go where we aren't wanted. I truly am the step child" he said with a laugh. "Neither grandma nor pop want us at their house. Too much trouble for them and the spouses I guess."

Forty years later and his parent's divorce as fresh as ever.

"We will never do this to you guys." Vicky said into the back seat.

Vicky turned to Joseph. "They really don't give a shit about you or the kids. Their parents helped them with everything, and they do nothing for you."

Truth. Joseph realized long ago. Parents are not infallible. They can be assholes like anyone else.

"What is funny." Joseph said with self-pity "is that the wedding they are blowing us off for is for my cousin Mike. My dad gushes over him because he owns his own business."

"What does he do again? I can't keep all of your cousins straight." Vicky asked.

"I don't know, I think he owns some carpet company.

***

"Why are they like that?" Vicky asked.

Joseph was reading his book in bed.

"It's like you said. They each got remarried and have their own kids now. Plus we are a big family. When we come to town it puts them out I guess. Whatever, I really did not want to drive up there anyway. And like I said in the car, I really think my dad just doesn't understand me and he doesn't like my career choice. He would rather be with family he understands, like my cousins. They are just like him. Uneducated blue-collar guys..."

"Yea," Joseph wasn't sure, but he thought he saw a smirk from Vicky.

"Well, I guess you were right all along about them." He said a little vindictively.

"Its both our parents." She said defensively.

"Yea, but we still see your parents." He said.

"Don't blame it on me!" she began to raise her voice. "Its not my fault. You were the one..."

"I know," he said quickly. "Its not your fault we aren't seeing them, but you never liked them so you are getting what you want. Plus, you get to say I told you so."

"Can you please stop." She said. "We just know what to do when our kids are older."

"Yea and it just makes your parents look that much better." He said spitefully.

"Well, at least they visit us." She said flatly.

Joseph did not have a good retort to this because it was true.

"Well, I am sorry my parents do not love me enough to come to see me or want me to see them. We can just go see your parents and they can tell me what an asshole I am because I have a college degree."

"Why do you make everything about them and your degree?" Vicky blasted him back.

He sensed he was kind of being an asshole, but all the hurt overwhelmed him. Its hard to find out your parents do not want to see you. Most animals do abandon their children at some point. All that was left were severed connections in a lonely universe,

"I know. I am sorry. Its just your parents are the only ones that half give a shit about us, but I still am irritated with how they treated me in the past." He said.

"Well, you said it got better right? They don't treat you like that anymore?"

"Yea, it is better. But..." He paused. "I wonder if its because I take care of you."

"What do you mean?" she asked. He could hear the oil furnace kick on downstairs.

"They only really started treating me better a few years ago, which coincided with you taking a turn for the worse."

"So?" she asked. In the darkness he could see she had squinted her eyes and cocked her head when she asked him this.

"Because, maybe they didn't want to piss me off. They realized that you are getting worse and that I take care of you. If I didn't take care of you, what would they do?"

"Again, what do you mean?" she said impatiently.

"You would be in a home without me." He had never said that to her. It was the truth, but it was harsh.

"Really?" she said, offended.

"It's the truth. You would be in a home without me or they would have to take care of you. You cannot take care of yourself." And that was true, she could not work, drive, handle money, cook or even shop. She had a difficult time just walking to the bathroom.

"Your parents could help too, but we know they won't." She said defensively.

"True." He said. "They don't do shit, as evidenced by what just happened today. But if something happened to me, you wouldn't be their responsibility. I think your parents have only gotten nicer to me because they know I take care of you. I may not be the best caregiver, but I didn't leave you and I don't cheat on you."

"Do you want a fucking medal?" She asked indignantly.

Temporary Gods and Arbitrary Arrangements

"No, I don't." He took a breath. "But you need to understand I am not some savior. You, your parents and everyone else want me to perform miracles and be superman and take care of you and you just keep getting worse." He saw her frown when he said this. "I am just a normal guy, I am not a savior, I can barely take care of myself and these kids. You require so much work."

"Don't you love me?" she asked with tears beginning to well in her eyes.

"Of course, but this isn't some movie where love conquers all. There are real concerns here. You need round the clock care. I am not a nurse or a paid caregiver. You don't get training for this."

"You think this is easy for me?" she shot back. "You think you get trained on how to be sick? How to basically lose your ability to walk? I don't feel sorry for you!"

"Fair enough. And you are right. But this is not about anyone feeling sorry for me. All I am trying to tell you is that everyday you get worse, and I feel like I have to do more and more and your family just expects me to shoulder this without any help. I don't think they have ever even said thank you. I need help. I need someone here to drive you to your doctor visits, call the insurance company and shit like that. You can't even walk up the front steps anymore. And frankly, I don't know if you would do the same for me." This is something he had thought long and hard about. He just wasn't sure if she or anyone would take care of him.

"Of course, I would!" She said defensively.

"You say that, but you really just don't know. When I was writing my dissertation, and you had to do some extra stuff for me, I felt like you always got annoyed."

"That is not true!"

There really was no point in arguing about this, and it even it was true, it was no indicator of what she would do if the situation was reversed.

"Maybe, but you never know."

There was a long period of silence between them.

"I am sorry I am such a burden." She said as she rolled over.

He did not say anything else to her.

Chapter 9
Year: 2030

Joseph drank more coffee and finished his breakfast. He sipped the last sip and went to refill it. The hospital probably did not offer free refills, fuck them. He took the free coffee *and* more milk and sat back down. He just screwed this hospital out of $2.76 while they screwed him out of $80,000. No one said anything to him as he returned to his seat. He finished grading the essays and inputted the grades. It wasn't $80,000 but it was a lot. He had been pouring over the documents and bills. He wasn't sure how he was going to pay for it all, coupled with his mortgage and some of the college loans he had taken on for the kids. The health insurance-industry '*industry*', that is exactly what it was, an industry didn't produce anything. It didn't create any medicines or heal anyone, no, instead it was like the mafia with ties and MBAs. One of America's greatest inventions was to develop an apparatus to fuck hardworking people out of their money. But what could he do? He remembered the lyrics to a Smashing Pumpkins song:

"Despite all my rage/I am still just a rat in a cage."

That line encapsulated his entire life. Rage, anger resentment, these things had grown, festered as he aged. The goddamn cage closed in around him, year by year. And almost on cue, he heard a shrill voice emanating from the T.V. like the voice of some arrogant God.

"We are here today to make America better! This historic tax cut will bring jobs back to America, it will enrich the middle class. The trials against me were a distraction, but I have prevailed, for all of you..."

"It will enrich those that already have enough." Joseph said to himself. Joseph put on his headphones. He could not listen to this drivel. Like some Buddhist monk, he just wanted to disengage from the world and live in a mountain cabin.

Almost like a preplanned script, as soon as that politician was finished, the news station cut to another well-known face.

"My opponent believes..."

Joseph writhed in his seat even though he was no longer listening. Like a fucking rat in a cage. Both of these politicians had been accused of various crimes, and while it is innocent until proven guilty, everyone knew they had done it. There was incontrovertible evidence, but it did not matter. Like all powerful men, they were able to evade any sort of accountability. There is no accountability in the universe, no justice, there is no deserving, there is *no* level playing field, there just *'is.'*

But then he remembered the philosophy papers he was grading, and in some way, they always gave him a strange comfort. These stupid clowns on the television, rich and powerful people who pretended to have Americans' interest at heart, were all charlatans. They grew fat and rich while the majority of people just got by, or suffered. Most did not give a shit about the people they represented. But that is where philosophy comforted him. He read Plato and Nietzsche, he read history, and he understood that America was not the first to be duped, not the first country to have bad leaders.

In some way or another, this state of affairs had existed since the beginning of the written word and probably before that. It's like some celestial script, where we're told who to hate, who to love, where to go, what to vote for. And now the scripts were even more elaborate. Like rats in a cage who could press the lever for pellets. And when the pellet tumbled down into the tray we celebrated our own ingenuity and freedom.

Joseph noticed a man sitting a few tables down from him in the cafeteria. The slovenly man easily weighed over three hundred and fifty pounds. A rough scraggly beard lined his heavy face. Rolls of neck fat violently shook as the man clenched his face in agreement to the politician on the television. His lips curled into a sneer and his eyes narrowed, almost transfixed by the image on television. Drops of coffee spilled out of his cup which he gripped with white knuckles. Joseph saw the man wore a hat and shirt in support of the politician who ad passed the tax cuts which would most assuredly not impact this man in any substantial way.

Apparently, this is what progress looked like. The shirt had a giant middle finger on it and said, "Fuck the other side." The shirt looked worn, like the man had worn it for days without washing it. He imagined the man smelled of body odor but did not want to get close enough to find out. The shirt had a hole just below the man's right nipple and a small patch of pasty white skin beamed out. In front of him on the table were three plates of half eaten food, the stub of a jelly donut, a pile of French toast with little bits of syrup that intermittently dripped onto the glass plate, and some pieces of bacon on the third plate.

Joseph looked down at another student's essay, this one written on Thomas Jefferson. He then looked up at the man again. Joseph shook his head disgustedly. He half hoped the man would catch his look of disgust and say something, but then he checked himself. Punching out some illiterate piece of white trash while your wife died upstairs would not be very professional. Joseph had to swallow his rage like he had choked it down so many times before.

When he finished grading his papers, he packed up his laptop. Unfortunately, he had to walk right past the slovenly man to exit. And when he did walk past him, Joseph almost gagged from the overpowering stench of body odor and cigarettes. He turned back and saw the man staring at the television.

Chapter 10
Year: 2025

    She looked like a turtle that had landed upside down on its shell. Her legs kicked fruitlessly at the air, her arms helplessly waved at nothing. Her face contorted and a large spot of blood grew on the carpet. He had heard the unnatural clunk-clunk-clunk as she tumbled down the steps. When the laundry room door had flung open after her head smashed into it, a little decorative wooden plaque which read *"Love Starts Here"* thudded on the floor and skidded behind the wastebasket. Joseph stood at the top of the stairs and looked dumbly at Vicky for what seemed like a minute as she struggled on the worn carpet, the blood now forming a halo of sorts around her head. When he regained his senses, Joseph quickly rushed down the stairs and helped his wife sit up.

"I don't know what happened..." she said. "I...I...think my sock caught on the carpet and my feet just slipped out from underneath me and I tumbled."

Like a forensic detective, Joseph quickly scanned the wall and saw where she had banged her head. There was a slightly raised corner from a piece of molding which lined the bottom of the stairs. It looked liked her forehead had slammed into that during the fall.

"I think I am okay..." she sounded dazed.

"Are you fucking kidding me? We have to go to urgent care. Now. You need stiches." Joseph said as he helped her up. He might not have said that a few years ago, but one time his youngest daughter had taken a similar fall and split her eyebrow open. He stood there dumbly until another parent had suggested he take her to the emergency room. The gash on his wife's head was similar. Experience is a good teacher.

"No, I don't" she said weakly.

"Let's go." He walked her up the steps and crumpled up a paper towel. "Hold this on your head with pressure."

"Okay, but I need my coat."

"Don't worry about your coat! Jesus who gives a shit! It is like 70 degrees outside!" He grabbed his keys and wallet and walked her to the door.

"Godammit." He said. "Where is my phone?" But then he saw it on the glass shelves in the kitchen which were supposed to be a display for nice keepsakes but had turned into a docking station for all sorts of random crap.

"I need my phone too." She said.

He wanted to blow up on her again. She had bled through the paper towel. He quickly scanned the kitchen table and saw her phone. He grabbed it and another handful of paper towels.

"My cane..." she said.

In one sweeping motion he opened the door, got her cane, stuck it in her hand and walked her down the steps and got her situated in the car. He started the car and drove to urgent care.

Temporary Gods and Arbitrary Arrangements

The sign-in process was laborious. They had been here a number of times. A few weeks ago, he had to take her to urgent care for an infection on her finger. A few weeks before that she had been sick. Since she could not drive herself, he felt like a medical taxi. He began the sign in process and then they waited for almost an hour. Finally, they were admitted in. He feared the nurses might think he beat her. She needed to answer the questions but half the time she looked like a deer in head lights.

"Hello ma'am. What happened?" the nurse asked pleasantly but concerned.

"I...my sock caught on the step and I fell down the steps and hit my head."

The nurse looked at Joseph to confirm the story and Joseph nodded. "I didn't see it, I was on the couch and heard the fall. She has MS and takes a lot of falls." He said, almost defensively.

The nurse cleaned up the wound and then examined it. The room seemed abnormally warm. Every time Vicky shifted on table's soft plastic surface, it sounded like little farts. If his wife wasn't bleeding he probably would have laughed.

"It looks like you will need about four to five stitches." For some reason Joseph noticed all of the used up wadded gauze pads in the metal tray. Like a snow storm. He wondered if the nurse heard the little plastic farts.

The nurse applied lidocaine and a local anesthetic. She then began to suture the wound. It took five stitches.

"You will need to come back in a week for us to remove the stitches." The nurse said. "I will send in a prescription for painkillers to your pharmacy."

Joseph walked Vicky to the car and they drove home. The air had cooled down and the October moonlight streamed in the car and illuminated alternating sections of the black leather seat.

The falls had become more frequent now, but they had not risen to this level until now. Vicky always took little stumbles but this was the first time a fall resulted in a trip to urgent care. Tripping hazards and obstacles of all sorts cluttered the house which required them to undertake a process similar to babyproofing it

Joseph dispensed the painkillers to his wife and put her to bed. She fell asleep almost instantly. Joseph looked at her, with the stiches on her head, a little puddle of drool leaked out of her mouth. This once strong athlete, this once curvy and voluptuous woman, whom men would hit on and buy drinks for (some she would take home and some she wouldn't), was now pathetic. Her bones jutted out of her skin awkwardly. She still had some of her figure, smaller but still shapely breasts poked out of her t-shirt and he could see the curve of her butt under the blanket. But the damage had been done. Like some aging dog that now limped along, or a horse with a broken leg and struggled over the finish line, like an old, neglected muscle car, rusted out with broken bearings.

He thought of something he read many years ago in one of his undergraduate literature classes, something about the "human condition." This is our curse as humans. Youth, health and beauty fade. In an instant, your joints ached and eventually stopped working. Your bones became brittle, or you contracted MS. and became bedridden, a shell of your former self where all you could do was remember.

There were no instructions or painkillers for the human condition.

Chapter 11
Year: 2028

The ball bounced around the rim a few times. Joseph's heart felt like it didn't move. Finally, the ball dropped through the hoop and the points were awarded.

"Yes!" he cheered loudly. "Great job Bridgette!"

His daughter gave him a quick look and nodded her head as she ran down the court. A player from the other team tried to pass to a teammate but Bridgette, who seemed to come out of nowhere, stole the ball and glided down the court. Another basket. Joseph pumped his fist in the air. She scored again, 6 points in less than 3 minutes. They won the game by 3.

Twelve-year-old girls' basketball might not be interesting to most people, but for

Joseph, it became a symbol. He watched his daughter steal the ball, make shots and effortlessly glide down the court, he watched Bridgette and really all of his children accomplish feats he could not dream of, Joseph realized that he might be witnessing evolution in real time. His children evolved past him but not in a Darwinian, survivalist sense but perhaps in a spiritual sense. They all surpassed him to become something else, something better. So did his students.

But, still, Joseph could still remember his grandmother always chastising him.

"Why do you care about sports so much? This is all meaningless!" she' say. And in some sense, that was the truth. Sports are meaningless. Joseph wrestled with this for a long time until he finally realized something. Sports were indeed meaningless, but so is everything else. And if everything is just as meaningless, then this basketball game could perhaps was becoming the most important and meaningful thing in the entire world because he, Joseph, wanted to invest it with meaning. If there were no God, no purpose, there were just basketball games and guitar solos and poems. Every poem written and basket made was a type of spiritual evolution. Joseph was not as good as his daughter, she was a better athlete, smarter, all of his children had achieved so much, they were evolving past him.

"You played great!" Joseph walked over to his daughter when the game ended. Vicky clung to his arm as he she put her cane out in front of her when she walked.

"Thanks Dad. Did you see my steal?"

"Yes! Amazing!" Joseph said.

"You were great!" Vicky said.

Joseph also knew that when his wife watched Bridgette play any sport, she saw herself as she used to be, before the MS, before the human condition. The children were the better part of the both of them.

Bridgette sat at the table with her cheeseburger and her juice. She voraciously chomped at the meat; she had the right to after the way she played. A few crumbs from the bread sprinkled on the wrapper. A little piece of yellow cheese remained on the wrapper as well.

"You really were great today." Joseph told his daughter, "But more importantly than baskets and steals, you showed mental toughness."

"Yea, I made some mistakes in the beginning of the game, I felt like I could not hit a shot, I wasn't perfect, but I kept on playing." Bridgette took a bite. "Then I started to feel good, and the baskets just kept coming. And then, everyone else started playing well." Bridgette said as she finished the last swig of her juice.

"That is leadership." Vicky said.

Bridgette smiled at her mom.

"Can I get some more juice from the machine?" she asked

"Of course." Joseph said with a grin.

Bridgette got up from her seat and refilled her juice. Joseph watched her, the basketball uniform slightly too big as it drooped off her shoulders a little. Her hair pulled back into a tight pony tail. Joseph helped Vicky to her feet as she collected her cane. She latched onto his arm and all three of them walked to the car. It was raining, but they hardly noticed it; all three of them were happy.

Chapter 12
Year: 2023

It looks like the circulation pump is shot." Peter said with a muffled voice from inside the dishwasher cubby.

Joseph didn't know the circulation pump from a lamp post.

"Okay." Joseph said dully.

"Can you hand me that red screw driver?" Peter asked in the muffled voice again.

Joseph rummaged through Peter's tools and found the red screw driver and slid it into the black hole of the dishwasher cubby.

"No, I need the other red one."

Joseph retrieved it.

Joseph stepped into a small puddle of dirty dishwater and his sock was instantly soaked. He rolled his eyes but no one saw.

"We are going to have to go to Lowes." Peter said. "Because we need more wire."

"Okay," Joseph said, "I can drive."

Peter scooted out of the cubby hole. Patty, his wife, sat at the table and took a sip of coffee.

"You should have seen him last week!" Patty exclaimed as she set her mug back on the table and gestured toward her husband triumphantly.

"Lynn and Allan's water heater burst in the middle of the night. Allan was able to shut the water off and clean up some of the mess. They called us in the morning and Pete had it fixed by afternoon.

"Is Allan not that handy?" Vicky asked as she leaned forward.

"Oh no!" said Patty with gusto. "Ever since Lynn and Allan have been married, Pete always had to do things for them around the house. Pete redid their garage, fixed their toilets, water heaters, you name it!"

"Wow," Vicky said with her eyes wide. "It's good to have you around." She said to her stepfather.

"Yea, and Lynn and Allan's son came over to try and help," Patty continued. "He is supposed to be really smart, he has a master's degree, works for NASA or something, but even he couldn't figure it out. Pete had it fixed in two hours. They bought us a case of beer." Patty finished her coffee.

"They don't teach that stuff in school and they probably should." Pete said.

Joseph cracked his knuckles. They popped but he kept baring down on his knuckles, almost pulling them out of the sockets. He bit the inside of his cheek.

"This is why..." Pete condescendingly said, "I am really glad John and Olivia are homeschooling the kids."

Joseph seethed with rage but did not speak. He did not take the bait.

"Yea, this way they can teach them useful things." Patty said in agreement.

"And schools in their area are pretty bad." Vicky chimed in.

Joseph gathered his keys and wallet. "Should we go now?" Joseph asked flatly. They could probably tell he was annoyed.

"Okay." Pete said.

Joseph did not disagree at all with homeschooling, it certainty was appropriate for some students, but when the people who were supposed to be your teachers barely graduated high school themselves that did not bode well. And of course, no one ever consulted Joseph for advice, despite the fact that he held a PhD in education.

The haughty way her family sat around and condemned his livelihood, his interests, his knowledge lit a fire in him, it awakened something he had never felt before. He never felt so useless before.

He could not fix things or work with his hands, but he always believed he had his sphere of knowledge and thinking, philosophy and literature and he would be respected for it despite his lack of handy skills. But he quickly learned otherwise. From politicians to his in-laws, to his own father, he became the butt of everyone's joke. They held him in low regard, saw him as useless. This never dawned on him until he had been married for a few years. And in some ways, he had to agree. If your sink was leaking you do not call a poet. If you need a tire changed, you do not call an author. No, you call people who can work with their hands. What could he do? Give you an analysis of T.S. Eliot? Talk about lesson objectives and pedagogy while someone more mechanically inclined fixed the engine? He was not useful, at least in a practical sense. He had always believed that he was valuable, useful in a more existential sense, but after a few years of marriage to Vicky, he was not sure. Her family were salt of the earth type people, who grew up far away from cities and urban areas. They farmed and hunted and repaired old tractors. They didn't go to college and they didn't read poetry.

"I am really glad Pete fixed the dishwasher." Vicky said that night in bed.

"Yea, it probably saved us about $600 dollars." Joseph said. Much to Joseph's chagrin, this was correct.

But at the same time, he didn't believe himself a complete failure either. Joseph had written some books, he was a good teacher, and a capable administrator. Most importantly, he could support his family on one salary. A failure was someone like his uncle Greg, who succumbed to drugs early on in his life, who was in an out of jail, who had to be supported by his family, namely Joseph's father. At the last, he heard, Gabe was living in his father's car shop, sleeping on a goddamn cot in the middle of the fucking office with a space heater because he could not hold a job. That was a failure.

Joseph was not a failure, but he also wasn't a total success either. He was a good teacher, but not a great teacher, all of his colleagues had been given prestigious teaching awards while Joseph had never won anything. While he had published books, as one of his colleagues reminded him, in their profession, books do not count, research articles do.

He had published some research articles, but not in any high-ranking journals. And while he had some important administrative achievements under his belt, he was not cut out to be a real leader, his administrative achievements were small potatoes compared to his colleagues. They had engineered grants and large programs. He had made some small changes which would probably need to be scrapped of modified beyond recognition in a few years.

He was not a failure, but he wasn't really a success, he was sort of there, hanging on, average or maybe slightly above average, but he had the sober realization that in this universe, where configurations were random, nothing he accomplished would outlast him, he could not create meaning.

"Maybe you should have married someone like him." Joseph said with slight annoyance. Being handy is like a goddam religion in your family. If you have a PhD you are an idiot and an asshole, but if you can install a water heater you are Jesus Christ"

"Stop, not this again" Vicky said.

"Its true." You are so proud of him.

"Don't be jealous because your career did not pan out the way you thought it would." She stared at him, a little surprised at herself for saying the obvious out loud.

This was true, and he and she knew it. He took his time before responding.

"Like your family is any better? A bunch of uneducated illiterate rednecks. Maybe I didn't quite get to where I wanted but, I write books, I am an author and a teacher. What have they done? What have you done? You were a good athlete, like what, 20 years ago?"

He could not believe he said that.

"I am sorry I got sick."

"Yea, and whose fault is that?"

"It's not my goddam fault you asshole!." She shrieked. "Its not because I fucked too many people! I got MS., I am genetically predisposed to it! You are not a fucking doctor, a real doctor anyway!"

She loved to throw that fact in his face. He had a Doctor of Philosophy, far off from an MD. That did not matter right now though.

"I am sure all of the drinking, smoking and fucking you did in college had no effect whatsoever. And now I have to take care of you!"

Both of them remained silent and seething in the moonlight. Vicky collected herself.

"Tomorrow, he is going to fix the light switch." Vicky said dully, not acknowledging the grenade Joseph lobbed at her.

Joseph should be able to figure out how to fix a light switch. It was another way to passively-aggressively insult him, which she had done for years. Watch YouTube like all the handymen told him. He tried watching videos of things online but it never worked. He still couldn't figure it out. At this point he had just ceded this sphere to Vicky's family. They knew how to fix things, he did not.

He'd had a flurry of brief activity, talking with his friend and learning how to do some basic carpentry and plumbing. And for a brief second Vicky's family respected him, even taking his design for a railing and building a similar one for a disabled friend. But that faded. And Joseph just did not have the energy to keep repairing things, and building and fixing. He just did not care any more.

The universe frayed and broke more every day. Let them fix the world. He just wanted to read, just write things that no one will read. He wanted to be a moderate success and no more, a minor poet, forgotten soon in a world with no meaning.

"Okay that is great. I have some grading I have to do tomorrow." Like the insults never happened.

"Can you help him though?" she asked.

"I should have some time, but I do have a ton of grading to do." Of course, he could spare the ten or fifteen minutes it would take to help, but wanted his dignity.

"Well, they came all the way from Florida to help us."

"I don't really help him. I just sort of hold his tool belt. I think he likes the fact that I have a college degree, a few degrees, but have to rely on him to fix these things."

Vicky sighed.

He rolled over without saying good night.

What does a philosopher or poet fix? Maybe the universe? In a larger sense, he believed he simply made observations about their new configuration, new terms of attachment.

Chapter 13
Year: 2027

She had only her underwear on. The faded purple pair with the two holes under the elastic band. Her smaller but still shapely breasts flattened slightly as she laid on her back.

"What do you want to do?"

A steady cadence echoed throughout the room as rain pelted the window. Through the small slit in the old curtain, which she made sure Joseph had pulled tight over the window, he saw grey sky and it comforted him.

Joseph did not answer but began to kiss her breasts and then moved to her belly. It bore the marks of their three children, there were stretch marks and lines, and the belly was no longer smooth, she had taken her belly button ring out long ago. But this never detracted from her looks, in fact, Joseph thought it made her sexier. She had life stories, she had experience, children. He slowly moved down and began to kiss her belly button. She threw her head back and gripped the sheets tightly.

When they finished, and she had recovered, she rolled over onto her belly. Joseph parted her hair and kissed the back of her neck. He then kissed her shoulder blades and worked his way down to her lower back.

***

They laid naked in the bed.

"I need to fold that laundry" she motioned with her head to the pile on the floor.

"Yea, and I have to take out the garbage.

Sex reminded him of a quote from the Roman emperor Marcus Aurelius, who said something like sex is just the rubbing together of two bodies until semen comes out. Nothing glorious or romantic, just another thing we do as humans. In addition, after sex, you need to do laundry. You fuck, but you also need clean clothes. Maybe the universe used sex to trick people into joining together, the universe finding a way to create new arbitrary arrangements, which in turn created some temporary meaning.

He still resented her but also wanted to get laid, so he had to put those feelings aside. But now they returned. She slowly got dressed. She fastened her grey bra but this took a few attempts. She then unsteadily walked to the pile of laundry on the bedroom floor. Now that they were fully dressed, Joseph opened the curtains to let the grey light in. he noticed the curtain, from the previous owner, had a slight stain on it, presumably from rainwater. He never got around to changing it out. He looked out the window past his house into the surrounding hills. About two or so miles off, a large blue water tower jutted out of the landscape.

"We definitely do a lot more in bed now than we used too," she remarked as she folded a pair of her shorts.

"I guess I wore you down" he smiled.

"I think that happens with most married couples, you have to keep it interesting." She said as she placed the shorts on the floor. "I will let you do all this shit to me no matter how disabled I get."

"Yea, I read that somewhere. After twenty years, you gotta keep it interesting I guess. And don't worry, I will keep doing it to you."

He had just fucked a disabled woman and she told him that he could keep doing it, no matter how bad she got. He did not know how to take that. Morbid, but strange and exciting, the sexual urge is a powerful one.

"I wouldn't have let you do half the stuff you do now when we were first together." She grinned.

They had evolved sexually over the course of their marriage, like an ape or star or seed, their sex life had been transformed into something almost unrecognizable from the beginning. But this arrangement was temporary as well.

Chapter 14
Year: 2027

The email icon beeped and Joseph opened it to read:

Dr. Joy,
Unfortunately, the students you sent in forms for cannot be registered for this course.

The email came from the registrar. Half of Joseph's day he spent dealing with the registrar or the business office and usually over forms, rules and policies that he did not quite understand. Joseph, the Acting Assistant Dean, meaning that he was only filling in for a colleague who was on leave, had to navigate an unforgiving administration. He briefly glanced over to the copy of Kafka's *The Trial*, on his bookshelf and gave himself a sardonic grin.

"Why the fuck not." He muttered to himself when he reread the email.

He typed, hoping his annoyance would come through on email

> *Hello:*
> *I just received an email from the other registrar alerting me that all the students had been registered so I am confused. Please advise.*

He sent the email and waited. He debated forwarding the registrar's email to his dean, but that could lead to him having to track down more forms and send more emails. He was only the Acting Dean but was expected to understand every nuance of this arcane bureaucracy of which he did not. He only agreed to this role for the stipend. He was no leader.

And in a larger sense, this stint as dean had generated tremendous feelings of disappointment in him. He had not envisioned this for himself or his career, but here he was, haggling over stupid shit he didn't really care about because he needed the cash.

> *Dr. Joy:*
> *Unfortunately, the other registrar was mistaken. These students cannot be registered.*

"Goddam it." He said silently.

He had been tasked with getting these students registered even though he was not told this before hand. He forwarded the email to his dean with another added message

> *See email below. Registrar will not registrar them. Now what?*

He hesitated before sending this email because it made him look incompetent but he did not know what to do. He reminded himself that he was only the *interim* dean. He waited. His dean responded.

> *Tell them we have done this in the past, specifically the last two semesters.*

He wished his dean would send the email, it would have more gravitas coming from her. Instead he felt like a middle man. But he sent the email back to the registrar. He looked at his phone, 2:50, Friday afternoon. Maybe he could run the clock out on this thing, the registrar would be packing up at 4 o'clock, maybe earlier on a Friday.

Once he finally let go of his dream of a professorship at a larger research university, he opted for a smaller teaching school where he could publish things of interest to him, the downside was his work would largely be obscure and neglected. Which it had been for years. And he had to take up jobs he really didn't care about, like Dean.

Another email dinged:

Joseph
I don't agree with your choice of chair. Sylvia is too new at this and I am nervous for her. I don't think this is a smart choice, do you???

Sincerely
Krista Dekende

The disrespectful tone did not even faze him anymore. He had grown to used it. He did not pursue Sylvia as the chair and decided to ask someone else. Even though Krista had no power over him, she would just continually bitch and complain because that is what she did. He did not have the energy for a fight.

His dean wrote him back.

Use this form for each student and send back to the registrar.

Joseph looked at the form. There were over 150 students that needed to be registered. Easy, but tedious. Something a high schooler could do. He began to process the forms. Another email popped up.

Hi Dr. Joy
I do not see what assignments are due this week. Please advise

He responded quickly.

Hello Julie
Please check the syllabus for all dates.

He hoped some of his annoyance crept through that email as well.

Dr. Joy
Oh! I see them all now. Thanks.

The registrar emailed him back.

> *Dr. Joy*
> *Students can take this course however they will be charged a registration fee.*

Joseph shook his head in disgust. He knew this would also be a major issue. He forwarded the email to his Dean. In a few minutes, she wrote him back.

> *I will email the VP.*

Another unrelated email from his dean popped up in his inbox.

> *Greetings Faculty!*
> *It is my pleasure to announce the Milton Teaching and Fenster Research Awards! Without further ado...*
>
> *Milton Teaching: Krista Dekende.*
>
> *Fenster Research: Christine Larron.*
>
> *Next time you see them, make sure you congratulate them!*

Joseph stared at the email dumbly for a moment. Then, his anger began to well up, slowly at first and then rapidly. He knew he would not win either award. They were not prestigious, he had given up on winning any large awards outside of his university, but these two were annual awards given by his largely obscure university. Over the years, as his hope dwindled of winning any large award, and then of receiving and sort of recognition, he always held out hope of winning one of these awards.

Not this year.

And deep down he knew he did not deserve either award. The criteria for the research award depended largely on citations. He had some, but not as many Larron. And the teaching award depended on evaluations and, while he always had good evaluations, a strictly online teacher like himself had little chance of winning it, the award had been largely reserved for teachers who taught face to face. It irritated him that Krista won it, but she was a good teacher. What could he do? Another email popped up from his dean.

I got it resolved.

In three weeks, he would no longer be dean and he could not wait. He had given up on receiving any sort of recognition or praise. He just wanted to be forgotten, left alone in this cold universe, allowed to dissipate, dissolve into chaos.

Chapter 15
Year: 2030

"Dad."

Rita startled him when she opened the door to the room. He had dozed off again. She stood next to him and then sat down in the chair. He groggily opened his eyes, smiled and instinctively hugged his daughter.

"How are you babe?"

"Okay," she said as she handed him a small cloth bag.

"Another care package?" he smiled.

"Something like that," she smirked.

Joseph opened the bag which contained a small Ziploc bag of apples, some seltzer, a bag of walnuts, some Greek yogurt and skim milk.

"Thank you. Those parasites downstairs in that little grocery mart charge like $7.50 for a gallon of milk and double the price of yogurt." He put the milk and yogurt in the little mini-refrigerator.

"Bastards."

Rita couldn't help but smile.

"Still as cheap as ever."

"Frugal." Joseph smiled back.

"How is she?" Rita asked, almost out of habit because she knew the answer.

"Same" he said flatly. "How is school?"

"I'm taking a lit class right now that is killing me. You know I hate all that poetry stuff." She said to her father with a sly smile, knowing she was going to get a reaction.

"Oh c'mon, you're killing me." He said with fake sadness.

"Can you help me with some poems?" she asked.

"Of course." He said. "Let's see' em"

She gave him the poem:

The ape learns
To light a candle for his progeny
Who can speak new languages
Which he cannot understand
The ape watches his children
Play guitar and walk upright
His children build systems
And kingdoms and phylum's
To classify apes and amoebas
And the ape, still clutching his candle
Smiles
Even as his children
Cut out his brain
Because this is progress

"What the hell does it mean?" she asked with a smile.

Joseph read the poem a few times and turned it over in his head.

"What do you think it means?" he asked her back.

She shot him a stupid look.

"If I knew I wouldn't ask you. That is such a teacher question."

"Old habits die hard," He smirked.

"I don't know. I think it has something to do with growing old. Maybe watching your kids grow up or something." she said, "I don't know."

"I think you are on to something." He agreed. "Why do you say that?"

"Because" she said, "the ape is watching his children do things he can't."

"And what do his children do?" he asked

"They classify and categorize the ape, their father. And eventually they kill him in the name of some type of progress."

"Hmm," he furrowed his eyebrows. "Is killing your parents progress?" he smiled.

"Is that really the most appropriate thing to say?" She said with a sneer.

"I guess not. But I think you are correct. The poem is about the price of progress..."

"Or maybe the victims of progress." She said, "He smiled as his children killed him, so he was happy about dying, maybe because he thought he died for something."

"Maybe because the only person you want to surpass you is your child." He winked at her.

"Thanks dad. Are you hungry?"

"Starving." He enunciated the word. He grabbed his hat.

"Even with her dying you can only think of food." She said. There was a type of gallows humor between them which made them both feel better. They also knew that, were she conscious, Vicky would approve and join in.

"Let me get my coat." Rita walked over to the chair.

Chapter 16
Year: 2030

Joseph flipped open his laptop and booted it up. A new email popped up from a journal he had submitted to.

> *Dear. Dr. Joy*
> *Thank you for your submission to the Journal of Democracy and Education. Unfortunately, your submission is not the right fit for our journal...*

Not a surprise. He submitted to these journals more out of habit and lacked the ambition he once did, but every rejection stung a little. At least he had already signed a book contract for his book. Albeit, as his advisor told him long ago, research articles in journals mattered, not books.

The clacking of the computer's keys echoed strangely in the darkness. The snow fell silently outside while Vicky lay peacefully dying in the bed. No noise could be heard save for her life support machines at two a.m.- the spiritual hour. Joseph had written about half the book. A book that no one will seriously read. He had a small but modest citation record, some decent book sales, but he was relatively unknown.

He did not believe this book would change his profile much, but it would be his masterpiece. Using poetry to think about democracy, to reimagine democracy, and, when the time came, to surpass democracy. Joseph, with his education degree, was not a true historian or philosopher, nor did he ever feel like a true social scientist. He did not fit anywhere in this lonely universe, or at least in this temporary configuration.

"Poetry, now, becomes philosophy."

He looked at what he typed.

If poetry became philosophy, it would open up new doors, new ways of thinking. Perhaps we as human beings would not be locked into our rigid memorized grammatical and linguistic patterns; these constraints would no longer guide our thoughts.

Poetry transforming into philosophy, whatever that meant, would not appeal to many people and Joseph knew that. And Joseph realized even he did not foresee all of the consequences this change might mean and he feared he had not explained it well enough, but there it was.

It began to snow, hard. The white gusts whipped up like angry ghosts, slamming the windows with silent thuds. A far-off streetlight cut through the snow and darkness and created an eerie glow which somehow melded the natural look of the snow to the industrial hospital outbuildings.

It seemed so odd, writing about the death of democracy, but nothing lasts forever. He continually saw the incompetence, the stupidity of humankind, the burnt-out buildings, exorbitant insurance and pharmaceutical bills, the grinding, preventable poverty of millions, the corrupt politicians, the idiot celebrities and sleazy demagogues who cloaked themselves in patriotism only to enrich themselves at the public's expense.

How could a democracy be run like this? Was democracy ever even possible? He included himself in this morass, he was no savior, he was not special. What did he do? Not much, just authored books that no one will read.

At this moment, everyone on the planet could be fed, clothed and sheltered. But what did we, as a species do? Allowed millions to writhe in poverty while a few individual billionaires and multinational companies pulled the strings of governments and lose ourselves in sports and celebrity culture? It was fucking lunacy.

Joseph considered these questions and posed poetry as the answer. But not just poetry, rather, he meant the spirit of art, what poetry represented, unfettered creativity, a willingness to suspend logic. Again, he realized this would not appeal to most people, and he had a hard time believing it himself.

Poetry allowed him to explore something darker as well. Democracy is not static, it evolved, and his argument was that poetry could help guide it to something better. But if democracy evolved, could it devolve? And who would be the judge?

He swished his coffee around. Surprisingly, the coffee had not gone cold. He walked over to the window, opened it slightly and breathed in the crisp snow filled air that instantly filled his lungs. He exhaled into the night and watched his breath rise.

If Vicky were conscious, she would be angry at him right now for opening the window on a cold night.

But he needed some air. He closed the window and latched it shut and went back to his coffee. What would anyone care about his ideas and opinions of democracy? Who was he? Admittedly, a nobody. Other scholars ignored him, and this book would go unread. But he still believed he needed to write it, if only for himself.

Poetry can be many things, it does not have to be nailed down into any logical position. No, poetry, can continually give birth to new ideas over the course of generations. Scientific and empirical literature, democracies and marriages are just arbitrary arrangements in space that people use to make meaning, but poetry defies that rigidity.

Vicky and democracy maybe were dying together. But these were only cosmic blips. The slime molds and rocks and insects laugh at our democracies and marriages, they laugh at our order.

Maybe he could be a poem and evolve past this arbitrary arrangement...

He shifted the laptop and reclined back in the hospital chair. He still had about a half cup of coffee.

A nurse came in to the room.

"Oh!" She said in a startled whisper. "I didn't know you were in here Mr. Joy. I came to check on your wife and do my rounds." Technically, he should be addressed as Dr. Joy, but he had never corrected anyone on this since earning his doctorate 15 years ago.

"Sorry, I didn't mean to startle you." He said. "I was doing some work."

"Nice and quiet?" she smiled.

"Something like that," he grinned. The nurse looked a few years younger than him. She wore blue scrubs and white tennis shoes and her hair had been pulled back but a small blond strand hung loosely over her eyes. She brushed it aside. She had small, studded earrings which refracted white in the moonlight.

"I won't bother you, I'll be going."

"No, its okay," he said. "I was taking a break anyway."

"What are you writing?" she asked.

"It's for my job. I am working on a book."

"Oh wow. What is it about?"

Joseph did not want to give the long, complicated explanation. He didn't want to tell her that he no longer believed in democracy. He did not want to try and explain about the burnt-out buildings and all the rest of it.

"Well," he said, "in a nutshell, its about the state of democracy, here in America and really the world over."

"Wow. Sounds intense." She smiled. She walked over to the machines and checked the vitals. She then replaced the pillows on Vicky's bed and readjusted the settings on another machine.

There seemed to be an almost icy blue glare in the room. The snow continued to fall.

"I will let you get back to your book," she smiled at Joseph.

"Thanks." He smiled back at her.

As she left, the familiar thoughts rose in his brain.

"What if..." the blue glare intensified. What if he had married that nurse? What if he married someone else? What if he inhabited another arbitrary arrangement in the universe somewhere? When he saw a beautiful woman, this thought always cropped up. He supposed some of this was natural, if he could relive his life, and he knew what it had in store, if he knew Vicky would deteriorate so quickly, would he still marry her?

The Nietzschean dilemma of eternal reoccurrence had been cropping up as his wife's condition worsened. Nietzsche had posed the question, would you relive your life over, every heartbreak, every painful detail, would you live your life over without changing anything? If you answered yes, then you had "affirmed" your life and made it meaningful.

Joseph thought about the nurse, with the little blond wisp of hair that fell over her face in the blue moonlight. She was beautiful, stunning actually.

Yes, he would remarry Vicky, over and over. He also knew that the question had to be bigger than just he and Vicky. He would always remarry her because without her, he would not have his children. He may have had children, sure, but not his children now.

Despite how stunning and beautiful the nurse was, she could never be his. He owned this life.

He returned to democracy, and it too needed life support, a fucking ventilator, actually.

No, democracy, as we all knew it, needed to die. All things change and die, eventually. All human arrangements are arbitrary and temporary, they rise and fall with no discernable pattern and for no cause.

The heart monitor's beeping filled the room.

Chapter 17
Year 2030

The warm church had that sweet wood smell mingled with dust and paper from the hymnals.

Faintly, Joseph also detected the smell of incense and the whole scene instantly transported him back to childhood. The soft artificial light rested gently on the tabernacle and the altar. Joseph sat in the pew and listened to the barely audible hum of the radiator. The pew creaked as Joseph moved slightly. This did not just bring him back to his childhood, this *was* his childhood.

Maybe his grandfather would be sitting next to him when he turned his head, praying devoutly, intently focused on the altar, no doubt relishing the suffering of all non-believers who were roasting in hell at that moment. He imagined his grandfather, singing the hymns, belting them out to show his reverence. An image of the crocodile tears welling up in his grandfather's eyes as he took the Eucharist by the mouth (because if you took it by the hand you may go to hell) formed in Joseph's mind.

He could imagine the soft light shining off of his grandfather's bald olive-skinned head and creating a patch of white light on that weird canvass.

Dogma takes a long time to get out of your system, like a bad case of food poisoning. It had to work its way through you until you finally shit it out. Joseph had about shit it almost all out, but even now, as he relished his atheism, there were still remnants of his grandfather's Catholic dogma in his system. Maybe that is why he liked to sit in empty churches from time to time. He did not pray, but he loved the silence and the smell.

Joseph pitied his grandfather and looked at him as a simpleton. It took many years, but Joseph realized that Giovanni Sorrento was not a creative man, his entire world had been laid out for him. For Giovanni, a strict god created a nice and tidy universe eons ago, then he created Giovanni, Giovanni died and then soon the world would end, sinners be judged, and all the righteous would go to heaven. Done. Simple as that. Predetermined progress. Just a road you had to walk on.

Joseph did not want to be put in a box, he did not want his entire life, and the entire history of the world, to be planned out. That, and the fact so many Catholics and religious people in general were the biggest fucking hypocrites imaginable. Rich pastors pretended to preach the bible while people starved.

While no bible expert, Joseph understood the main gist of the book. If his twenty years of being forced to attend church when he was a kid taught him anything, he knew that Jesus, a transient beggar, did not care for money. "It is easier for a camel to pass through the eye of needle than for a rich man to enter heaven." Or something like that.

Joseph saw the priest open a door behind the altar and slowly approach him. Joseph instantly wanted to leave. He just knew the priest was going to talk to him. Joseph did not want to talk, he just wanted to be alone.

"Hello," the priest came over and stood near Joseph.

"Hi" Joseph gave him a curt smile.

"What brings you here, anything I can help you with."

"No, just wanted some peace and quiet."

"Is a loved one of yours here in the hospital?"

"Yes, my wife."

"I am sorry"

Joseph was looking for a time to exit. The priest began again.

"Many people find solace here. I am here if you want to talk."

"That's okay. "But thank you."

"Whatever it is, God can help."

Joseph felt an all too familiar rage. One that he usually suppressed. He wanted to grab the priest by his stupid black and white lapel and scream in his bearded face. Did the priest really believe some benevolent being gave a shit about us?. That sounded like a story told to children when it thundered and they were afraid of the storm. He thought of his grandfather, and the supposed progress which was laid out for everyone. Like a nice little trail marked with ropes and railings in the woods. Fuck that.

"Thank you." Joseph said, a hint of annoyance in his voice.

"Remember son, everything happens for a reason."

That phrase. That fucking phrase. No, there was no reason for any of this.

"I am sorry" Joseph said with a sarcastic laugh. "I just do not believe that."

"That is okay, we have different beliefs. The church encourages a diversity of thought..."

First off, his grandfather would laugh. His grandfather said there was only one thought. None of this diversity shit. Second, Joseph felt like an asshole, because he was about to yell at this priest, a well-meaning old man.

Temporary Gods and Arbitrary Arrangements

"No, I don't believe in any of this shit. I am an atheist. I don't believe there is some god with a white beard in the sky who is taking care of his flock."

The priest looked bemused, like he had heard this before. "And yet, you sit in a church."

Joseph had to admit that might seem contradictory. "I like the peace and quiet. It doesn't mean I believe." Joseph said.

Then what do you believe?" The priest asked. Do you believe this world, and all of existence, is simply an accident? Imagine if you were walking on a beach, and you saw a watch. Would you assume the watch had no creator? Wouldn't you assume that an intelligence had created it? With all its moving parts?"

These people were all the same. Joseph's grandfather had used the same exact parable.

"As a matter of fact, I do believe we are accidents. You ask about the watch, but why would a god have billions living in poverty? Kill infants in their crib? Send natural disasters?"

"Because..." the priest said

"Let me guess," Joseph interrupted. "There is a reason for all of that. No. I just cannot accept that. We, human beings, and this entire existence, are fucking accidents. Its all one big accident." He had never said that out loud to anyone before.

"Then how did we get here?" The priest asked with a cocky, self- assured smile.

The age-old question. How did something come from nothing? Of course, Joseph could not answer with certainty.

"I don't know exactly. No one does." Was all Joseph cold muster. "You don't know either."

"Of course, I don't *know*." The priest still had that grin. "I have faith."

"There are experiments, there are people trying to answer this question. And I think they are getting close." Joseph said, albeit unconvincingly.

The priest did not speak, just continued to smile. Joseph continued:

"I don't know what was there in the beginning, but I do know somehow, somewhere, something clumped together, eventually this clump became sentient, and evolved from little amoebas to flying fish and then to apes and finally to us. And sometimes these sentient clumps love each other, and sometimes they kill each other. It did not have to happen like this, it just did. No god did this, it just happened."

The priest tried to cut in, but Joseph would not let him.

"Maybe our brains are just the result of billions of years of evolution, or transformation, the right combination of ingredients to blend together to produce sentience."

"How could something come from nothing?" the priest repeated in arrogance.

"Maybe there was nothing in the beginning, but it had to expel the idea of something to be truly nothing..." Joseph could not find the right words, he became flustered and angry. "I don't know, but you want me to take so many things on faith, and I am not allowed to have one item on faith? I don't know and I am okay with not knowing. Unlike you, I don't have a reason for everything."

The priest tried to regroup his words, but Joseph was not done. "That accidental sentience is the key to it all," Joseph said, more to himself. "It can create hell, but maybe...maybe it can also imagine something better than itself."

"Well, that is God..." said the priest.

"No, God is not better than humanity. All god is, is what humanity could be. Humanity is afraid of its creative powers and hides behind some fictious being. God is simply an obstacle, a psychological impediment because we are too afraid to exercise our powers...Maybe, maybe..." Joseph's voice grew more confident..."what we do in life builds our capacity when we die, if we pray to some made-up god or chase useless things like profits, we stunt our spiritual capacity, death is liberation. You, and your stupid religion were right in a sense, that this life matters but not in the way you think. Nothing is predetermined, there is no god who picks and chooses who goes to heaven or hell. We are the only force, the more we think, create, write, understand, love, the richer our spirit grows, the more we can truly exist when our human meat comes off..."

The priest shifted uncomfortably.

But even Joseph had a hard time believing that one. No, humanity, even with its accidental intelligence, like a frightened animal, cowered before its true potential. And we were not the only thing with intelligence. Slime molds could join together and operate as an individual organism and then go back to being single celled organisms, wolves had much wider ranges than anyone ever thought, trees can talk to each other. Maybe, there were many accidental intelligences and we just thought ours the best.

"You sound like a Buddhist."

"Maybe" Joseph said, again, more to himself as he walked away.

Joseph left the church and went outside. His feet crunched the hard snow and the cold air on this clear night instantly filled his lungs. His breath rose in rings before him. Joseph reached into this pocket and fumbled for his lighter and the "It's a boy" cigar. The warm drag filled his mouth and he held it for a few seconds before exhaling. He repeated this a few times and smelled the familiar cigar smoke as it fluttered away and mingled with his icy breath.

A nurse hurried outside and walked across the parking lot. He watched the nurse walk away. She was middle aged but still good looking. Her blonde hair bounced gently because she walked hurriedly. She disappeared behind the side of the hospital building.

Joseph took another drag and thought about his conversation with the priest. Nobody won that argument. The priest probably thought Joseph a lapsed Catholic, a lost sheep that had strayed from the flock. Joseph could imagine the priest praying for his soul. Whatever. Joseph had never articulated what he had said to the priest out loud. He didn't know if he believed what he said, but one thing he believed is that we are accidents. A benevolent god would not have struck Vicky with MS., would not kill babies in their cribs, and none of this happened for a reason. Progress, and some orderly rational plan for the universe simply did exist. As horrifying as this prospect was it felt good to believe something.

Chapter 18
Year: 2030

Joseph had dozed off again, he was not fully asleep when the nurse jarred him awake.

"Get some saline into that tube!" the nurse yelled to other nurse, who appeared to be in training. The nurse in training fumbled with the tube but quickly got it all set.

Joseph realized Vicky was dying.

The doctor came in and quickly.

On some level, Joseph realized this might be a formality of sorts. She was going to die.

Joseph sat in the room for a long time after she had died. They wheeled the body out and cleaned the bed, but they let him stay there.

He would have to make calls, her family, his family and of course the kids. They knew she would die, but thought they might have some more time for the kids to get there. But Vicky died with only Joseph in the room.

As the doctor checked her vitals and administered some type of medication in a frenzy, he remembered a few strips of her brown hair kept falling over her eyes. He remembered the frozen look on her face, closed eyes, the lines that streaked and creased her face like a little canyons that ran from the corners of her eyes down her cheeks. Her exposed breasts flopped helplessly as the doctors tried to revive her.

But she died without speaking, without regaining consciousness. She died with her breasts, sucked dry from three children, exposed, her tongue hanging stiffly in her mouth but unable to make a sound. Joseph watched all of this, as if it were a dog being put to sleep, like a cracked eggshell thrown in the garbage, the yolk used up long ago. The human condition in full view, on a random Tuesday in January.

It began to snow and the room was cold and empty with no one in it.

"Hi," the nurse said softly. "Are you okay? The doctor said to let you sit in here as long as you needed."

Joseph looked up. "Thank you." He said. Without thinking about it, he began talking.

"We met in college, and...it's just strange. I've known her for over half my life."

"You were college sweethearts?" the nurse asked.

"Yes, and I feel terrible because when she got really sick, part of me...part of me almost...but now..."

"That is very normal." The nurse said. "I have talked with a lot of people like you. They just want the suffering to be over, but when it is, there is a hole."

"Yea, I think that is the best way to describe it. Sorry, I didn't mean to dump all of this on you." Joseph said. He did not cry, he just felt in shock, bewildered.

"It's really okay. Take your time." The nurse said.

He stayed in the room a long time. At some moments in their marriage, he resented Vicky, at some moments, he hated her. But right now, he did not know what he was going to do without her.

***

"When did it...how..." Rita's voiced trailed off on the phone.

"It happened early in the morning. The doctors came in when I was sleeping...I watched the whole thing...I..."

"We need to call the funeral home, we need to make all of the arrangements..."

"I know..." Rita said.

"I will call your brother and sister. Let me tell them." Joseph said.

"Okay," Rita said.

***

One good thing about death, it brings people together, forces them to come together, at least for a little while. All the families came, the children helped Joseph. Joseph realized it was the only time in the last twenty years or so that the families were together.

"Dad," Rita said. "She looks good." Rita gestured toward her mother.

"Yea, she does."

Ron came over. "Dad, I am going to open the other bag of prayer cards. We are running low."

"Okay." Joseph said.

Bridgette greeted her aunt, Vicky's sister, Olivia, as Olivia leaned over the casket.

Rob, Joseph's friend of over 25 years, and Joseph's best man at his wedding came over and hugged Joseph.

"Hey bro." he said softly.

"Hey." Joseph said.

"What happens now?" Rob asked.

"I don't know. I guess we bury her and then..." Joseph's voice trailed off.

"You want to come over maybe? We can get some beers later? Anything to get your mind off of this?" Rob suggested.

"Not tonight. But can we do it Thursday? I need to be with the kids tonight.

"Of course." Rob said. I will pick you up.

Chapter 19
Year: 2030

Joseph got into the car. The heat had been turned to high and it felt good. Rob and Joseph, at one time college roommates, drove to a nearby bar and ordered some drinks.

"Feels like old times" Rob said. "You okay? I know it's a stupid question, but I don't know what else to ask." Rob said sheepishly.

"Don't worry about it." Joseph grinned. "How long have we known each other? Thirty years or something?"

They sat in silence for a while, staring at the football game on the bar's television. A waitress came and dropped off two beers. The largely dark and empty bar gave Joseph a sense of peace. He could not explain why.

"So, there is no cure for MS.? Nothing?" Rob blurted out.

"No. There are some drugs which can stave off the worst effects for a while, but there is no cure. Once you get it, you're fucked." Joseph said as he drank. "We had her on those drugs for years. Who knows what they really did."

"You would think, with all of the medicine and technology available..."

"Yea, in the end, nothing helped."

"So, what did the doctors do for her?" d.

"In all honesty, not too much. They gave her infusions which stopped the lesions from growing but it was what it was. I just had to watch her get worse every day."

"Its funny, because I feel like we hear about cancer a lot more than MS." Rob mused.

"Its true. We do." Joseph said flatly. "Cancer is more profitable to study so more money is put into cancer research. I remember hearing something when I attended one of her MS. support groups. Someone said something along the lines of keeping people sick ensures they keep paying, so there is no real incentive to a find a cure. That always stuck with me."

"Holy shit, that is fucked up."

Of course, I don't know exactly how all the research works," Joseph said, "But I wouldn't put it past anyone. From dealing with her illness and hospital bills and insurance companies, I learned that people do not really give a shit. If you are sick, you are fucked, really, you are disposable and exploitable."

"Two more beers." Rob signaled the waitress. "I am sorry man. This whole thing sucks. I remember the first time I met Vicky. In fact, I think I met her before you." Rob smiled.

"Yea, didn't you guys have that intellectual history class together on Tuesdays? I think she said it was her sophomore year?"

"Yup, that's the class. When did you guys meet?"

"Not until senior year, in our teaching seminar." Joseph said.

"Oh wow, I didn't realize you guys met so late in college." Rob said, "I can't get that out of my head though, what you said. About keeping people sick so they keep paying. Do you honestly believe there is truth in that?"

"I don't know." Joseph said. "I mean, I know there are good people, good doctors and nurses and scientists, but I think sometimes its larger than any one person, and there is a web in which we are caught. All this progress and medicine, and we are still assholes. People want to get rich and they don't care who they hurt."

"And the people that hurt other people and rip them off, don't actually see or interact with those people." Rob said.

"Right, they are just numbers on a spreadsheet." Joseph said. "Vicky was just some number on a spreadsheet while the CEO of our insurance company made billions. Fuck all of them." He said. "So much for progress." He finished his beer.

"What do you mean?" Rob said.

"Nothing, I am just rambling. Do you care who wins this game?" Joseph gestured to the television, he was sick of talking about it.

Chapter 20
Year: 2032

The road looked white, a blazing tunnel of endless white. The sky dumped inches of snow on this already white tundra as Joseph tried to navigate.

"I can barely see the goddam road." He said to himself.

"There is no pain, you are receding/A distant ship, smoke on the horizon."

The Pink Floyd lyrics echoed throughout the car, and Joseph thought them appropriate for driving through this blizzard.

As he pulled into his driveway, he realized he'd left all of the outdoor lights off. Joseph silently walked to his front door. His feet crunched the snow.

He trudged up the walkway in the dark, his shoes crunched the salt he had thrown down earlier. The sound died in the snow.

The inside of his living room reminded him of his college dorm room. Pizza boxes, beer cans, dirty clothes. Like he reverted back to 20 years old. He sank on his couch. The moon caught a beer can. No wife, no kids, just this dark, cold room. But he didn't need any of that anymore.

Pink Floyd echoed. He needed to hear *Comfortably Numb* again, he needed to let those lyrics wash over him as they had done since he was 13 years old. He booted up his laptop.

Maybe, democracy is not the optimal form of government any longer. The simple reason is that as the electorate becomes more partisan, polarized and distrustful, as people increasingly turn to their own echo chambers and social media diets which are unknowingly and carefully curated by billionaires, tech tycoons and other influencers to sow discord and confusion, as public education is continually stripped of its critical capacity, attacked and defunded, and as rampant anti-intellectualism takes hold, people can no longer make informed choices. If people can no longer make informed choices, if they are duped with misleading and emotional appeals into voting for demagogues who will only fleece them of their livelihood and income, and if the alternative political parties really do not offer any true or effective antidotes to demagogy, then a new form of government must take hold.

He looked at what he wrote and wondered if he could actually publish this. Not that it would really matter, no one read his works anyway. He would die in obscurity, so fuck it.

While no one could ever know the entire truth, he believed he articulated something close to a truth. The vast apparatus of this social media universe that surrounded everyone, of this culture industry, had been deployed to deaden people, to manipulate them. He knew he pontificated, in both speech and print, but it didn't matter because no one really listened to him anyway.

Maybe we dwelled in Plato's cave. And it was not as simple as a small group of people oppressing a much larger group with a definite plan. No, Joseph realized the oppression was subtle, diffuse and complex. And there were also real problems that needed solutions. But these demagogues gave the people rage and simplistic, unrealistic answers, and those people gobbled them up. He, Joseph Joy, a nobody, a rat in a cage with no power, no agency, now rooted for this democracy to fail.

Joseph glanced over at his nightstand and his dog-eared copy of *The Grapes of Wrath*.

But maybe, maybe democracy had *never* worked. Maybe it was always a soothing fiction, something we repeated to our ourselves, we told ourselves how superior we were. In the end, a million nobodies like himself were at the mercy of parasites and gods and got to vote for superficial and illusionary changes.

Billions of years on this planet led to Joseph, sitting in his room, alone, presiding over the death of democracy, which was what? An instable and fickle configuration of people and ideas in time, one accidental arrangement of blood and anger which is supposed to produce meaning, at least temporarily. Just like an atom, marriage or a family. What had it produced? Maybe some noble ideas like equality and liberty, maybe scientific progress and literature, but in the end, people were just too fucking stupid, cruel and apathetic, and they destroyed the little progress this accidental configuration produced.

Jefferson got it wrong. Democracy is a sham. Always has been, even if this sham is the best we could do. But now the gig is up. All of these arrangements of bodies in space revolve like solar systems. But democracies, and marriages and families do not last forever.

Joseph poured himself a glass of whiskey and drank it slowly. He walked to the window and watched the snow begin to pile up in little eddies. His front lawn became a tundra where all things go to die.

At least the whiskey was warm

Chapter 21
Year: 2032

"Do you want another drink?"

"Yes please" Joseph said to the waitress flatly. "Thank you," he said, and she walked back to the kitchen.

Joseph swished the beer in his glass. The waitress also brought his cheeseburger. He poured ketchup on the fries, took a swig of beer, and began to chew his burger, dunking the burger in a huge pile of ketchup. The fries were a little cold but it was not worth the hassle of sending them back so Joseph ate them. Small dribbles of fat squirted out of the burger onto his chin and onto the plate.

"Hi, can I have this chair?" The woman had short black hair which curved toward her forehead. She had blue eyes and soft creamy skin which gently rolled over her face.

"Sure." Joseph said, only mildly interested. He had played this game before.

"Are you here alone?" the woman asked.

"Yes, I come in sometimes for a burger and a beer."

"I know," she said sheepishly. I come in too and see you sometimes.

"Stalking me?" he smiled.

"Maybe." She grinned.

He remembered something his in-laws had said, many years ago. *"No one wants to be alone."* He had not been with a woman since Vicky died, and he didn't think he would be, at least not for a while. But it was nice to talk to people.

"Can I sit down?" She asked.

Joseph didn't say anything but gestured toward the seat.

"My name is Danielle," she stuck out her hand.

"Joseph." He did the same. Time to make small talk. "Okay, so...what do you do, your job, I mean?" Joseph asked.

"I work for an advertising company. You?" She looked at him with her deep, dark and strikingly beautiful eyes.

"I'm a college professor." He said.

"Oh wow, where at?"

"A small school in the city, Wilhelm University."

"I know that school. I did my undergrad not too far from there, at Sowtown University." Danielle said as the waitress placed her drink down.

They talked for over an hour. Mostly small talk, nothing substantial. But it was nice to talk with someone. *No one wants to be alone.* Danielle reminded him of his girlfriend before Vicky. A funny brunette named Beth. She had a rounded face and big eyes. And at least for a while, her and Joseph had some good times. She was his first true everything, he remembered the warm nights in her bed, stroking her back during the spiritual hour, her cool damp skin. He remembered the moonlight outside. He remembered Beth in pastel yellow shorts standing next to her fridge on a warm May afternoon. He remembered picking her up and putting her on the counter and kissing her mouth.

"Do you want another beer? On me?" Danielle said.

"Sure, but I'll get the one after that"

No one wants to be alone. But could he be with another women? Beth had been his last before Vicky. Human connections are severed, become memories in the void.

***

"You were incredible!" Danielle flailed her arms and looked like she was about to swim in the flannel sheets. Joseph placed his hand over her breast. This was not supposed to happen .,, but it did.

"Where did you learn those moves...and your mouth...you..." Danielle turned her head into the pillow again.

He wanted to tell her that after thirty years of marriage, you learn a few things. It isn't like when you are young and selfish, no, you learn how to connect with someone sexually, spiritually...

Did he cheat on his wife?

No, she had been dead almost two years.

No one wants to be alone.

"I know you said you were married. She was a lucky woman if you could do that to her every night." Danielle said, her voice muffled a little.

Joseph thought about this. Sometimes he had felt Vicky did not appreciate what he did for her in bed, either that, or he wasn't as good as he thought. He never could tell. Maybe she had better before him, but Danielle enjoyed it.

"How long were you married for?" Joseph asked.

"Three years and then we got divorced. I don't have any kids."

"What happened," if you don't' mind me asking.

"I don't know. We were on and off again high school sweethearts. I had a few boyfriends when I went away to college, but after college, we found each other again."

"What is his name?" Joseph asked.

"Scott Pearson. He works for the town. I am sorry, I know you told me last night but I cannot remember... how long were you married?" she asked.

"Thirty years, three kids." Joseph said. "My wife died about two years ago."

Danielle sat up. "I'm sorry, I thought you were divorced like me." She said a little embarrassed. "Too much wine last night." She winced.

"It's okay." He said with a laugh.

"Am I...the first women...since" she trailed off.

"Yes actually." He smirked. "I hope I wasn't too bad."

"No, I wasn't kidding, you were amazing. Um, what happened? If, ah, you don't mind…"

"No, its okay." He said. "She was diagnosed with MS. after we were married ten years. For the next twenty years, she steadily declined, until eventually, she could not function. Her body basically broke down."

"I am so sorry." Danielle said again. "So, you took care of her."

"Yea. As the kids got older, they were a major help."

"I think its an amazing thing, you taking care of her. A lot of guys would have left."

"Thank you, but I wasn't the best caregiver. I could be a real asshole to her sometimes." He said with a twinge of regret. "But I never cheated on her or anything. I mean, I guess you wouldn't know if I was telling the truth."

"I believe you. You don't seem the type to do that. Danielle smiled. "Actually, something like that happened with my grandparents, well not the cheating thing, but my grandmother got really sick and my grandfather had to take care of her. He became really short with her, always annoyed and irritable. When we talked to him about it, he told us we had no idea what it was like, basically like taking care of a child and it wears you down."

"Yea, something like that." Joseph said. "But I could still be a real dick sometimes." He said sadly.

"How old are your kids?" she asked

"Ron is thirty, Rita is twenty-seven and Bridgette is twenty-three. They are good kids. Ron works for the government, Rita just finished her master's in journalism and Bridgette is a high school basketball coach and science teacher."

"That is awesome. Maybe I can meet them someday. Do you think they would hate me?" she asked.

"No, I think they will be okay."

"I never had kids. I was always working. Then, after the divorce, I had some relationships but...it just never happened. I sort of regret it now."

In the universe of her bedroom Joseph stiffened slightly. He grimaced and looked out the window. Danielle covered her nakedness and sat down at her desk. She began to comb her hair.

"So, what do we do now? Was this a one-time thing for you? I don't really like to do that. I have not been perfect my whole life in the sex department, but I try to stay in relationships and don't want to just fuck around. But I also understand if you need time to process. Last night just sort of happened."

Joseph continued to stare out the window. "Me either, like you said, it just sort of happened. But I would like to keep seeing you." He said.

"Same here."

No one wants to be alone.

Joseph had just initiated another connection with a stranger and created a new arrangement in the universe, just like Vicky had done with her former lovers before they were married, just like all the billions of people that come together, even temporarily.

Chapter 22
Year: 2032

"James Wordley is now one of the richest men on earth." The voice boomed from the television. Joseph could only watch.

"He has presided over monumental changes at the two companies he helped found." The voice continued. "More than this, Johnson Bradley believes that James should be allowed a governing stake not just in this country, but in the direction for humankind."

"Sir, your coffee,"

"Thank you," Joseph took the black coffee from the worker and paid the bill. He sat down at a far table and opened his laptop and began to put his headphones in.

He always wondered why rich people thought they should run everyone else's life. Just because you made a million dollars selling batteries or porn websites, for some reason, that was supposed to qualify you as a great leader…

"This is what we need!" A belligerent voice thundered next to Joseph and interrupted his thought.

"Huh?" Joseph said startled, and probably a little stupidly.

"This guy is what we need to run this country!"

The man had a mustache that resembled an upside-down U. His eyes were fierce and a little too close together which gave him a menacing detached look and his thick hair receded a little. Joseph did not want to get into a political shouting match in this café. He only stopped in to get a quick cup of coffee and do some work. He tried to avoid confrontation.

"Okay," Joseph said disinterestedly.

The man would not let up.

Temporary Gods and Arbitrary Arrangements

"This man..." he gestured toward the television "will save this country!"

Joseph let out sigh. If his degree and studies and training in leadership taught him anything, it was no one was a savior. Reality is too complex for any one person to effect change.

"I think it's a little more complicated than that." Dammit. Joseph took the bait. He could see the man furrow his brow. An intense look crossed his face.

"No, its not! Bradley Johnson will save this country. He is a businessman and knows what we need!"

"Okay, buddy." Joseph said in a patronizing way.

"The problem is..." the man roared "you watch the wrong news and believe all the lies about him!"

Joseph sighed and shook his head.

"Actually, I have half a brain and I understand how politics and change work" Joseph said condescendingly. "To think one person can effect total change is just naïve and simplistic. This guy..." Joseph pointed to the TV "is a fraud. He makes you think he can do all of these great things, but it's a sham. All he cares about is lining his pockets, and his cronies. If you look at his record and supposed achievements, its all smoke and mirrors..."

Joseph waited for the man's reaction. The man pounded his fist down. The little glass container with the sugar packets almost rattled off the table.

"Take it back!" the man seethed. "Bradley Johnson has done more for this country than almost all politicians combined!" A little vein began to emerge in the man's forehead. "It's those goddam immigrants! They take our jobs and our homes! Bradley is going to clean this country up!"

Joseph could not contain himself. "That is the dumbest thing I have ever heard. Johnson a billionaire, and he and his billionaire friends like Wordley, many who have not been elected, are now running the government. They do not give a shit about people like you or me. There are issues with immigration, do not get me wrong, but that is used to distract you. Immigrants are not taking your jobs, they are cutting lawns and picking fruit. You have to be stupid to believe all that. No wonder this guy is taking money from the public schools. He needs to keep you ignorant."

"You think you are so much better, smarter than everyone. I can't wait until Johnson puts you and all people like you into a goddam camp!"

"Then you wonder why we call you Nazi's" Joseph smirked.

A manager came over. She was about 24 years old, brunette and shorter than both men.

"Is there a problem gentleman?" she asked nervously.

Joseph came back to reality. He did not want to scare this poor girl.

"No ma'am. I am sorry. I was just leaving." He packed up his stuff and left.

The other man glared at him as he left the café.

When Joseph went outside a blast of cold air hit him and made him shiver. He fixed his coat and walked down the sidewalk, which was covered in a grey slush. Bits of trash, dirty snow and dogshit covered the concrete.

For most of his professional career, Joseph had pondered the idea of progress and, more recently, decline. How did a nation, a people, a family or an individual progress? How did they decline? Did they know they were in decline? Joseph could not help thinking that man was a symptom of decline. Just like the fat man he saw in the hospital.

But he, Joseph Joy, perhaps, is also a symptom of decline, a breaking of an arrangement, a nobody, a celestial appendix. Perhaps we were all like an appendix, a useless growth that needed to be removed.

He walked into another coffeeshop. The warm air hit him as he took off his coat.

"A black coffee please." The barista handed him a cup. He put a little skim milk in it, found a table in the back of the café and sat down. The television was on, tuned in to the same station. Joseph saw the same face beaming from the television.

"Experts. Academics. Supposedly learned people...they are idiots! What do they know? Don't go to college! You don't need to..."

Joseph quickly put his headphones on. More anti-intellectualism. His family loved it.

Two men sat three tables down from him. They were skinny, had multiple piercings and wavy hair. They both looked similar. As the familiar candidate roared on television, they made faces of disgust.

While he probably agreed with these guys politically, he still couldn't shake the feeling that he played out some sort of prewritten script, that someone or something pushed him into certain positions of agreement and opposition.

It was a nagging feeling, that there was a binary situation and he was ordained to play one part or the other, by a higher power he did not fully understand.

The vast media and cultural apparatus were like a stone hung on him, on everyone. He dutifully played his part. But maybe that only held for this configuration.

Chapter 23
Year 2032

"What should we do with her stuff? I found another box of pictures and keepsakes." Ron asked as he set down a large plastic bin.

"I do not want to throw it out. Just make a pile, I want to keep it all." Joseph remarked.

Joseph began to sift through the box of Vicky's belongings. Old prom pictures, diplomas, athletic awards, certificates and trophies. A forgotten life lived and cataloged, like a dead star or fossil.

"Do you want me to put it in the attic?" Ron asked.

"Yea, if you could, my old knees don't like to bend to get into the door." Joseph smiled.

"Yea no problem old man." Ron smiled teasingly at him.

"How are you doing?" Joseph asked his son.

"As good as I can I guess. Keeping busy with the new job."

"How is it going?" Joseph asked.

"It's good. I'm in charge of a new project. We're mapping out new areas with the drones and I am team lead. We have these old maps from the 1930s with now abandoned mines and I have to transfer the data to new maps."

Joseph had no idea how to create a map on the computer and no idea how to fly a drone. He could never do what his son does.

"I couldn't do any of that." He grinned at Ron. "That is really amazing, great."

"Again, it's because you're old and can't work technology." Ron said jokingly.

"Truth." Joseph said flatly. "I'm just an old philosopher, and not a very good one at that."

"How are you doing with it all?" Ron asked.

"Like you, as well as I can."

"I talked with Rita, and she wants all four of us to go out to dinner."

Joseph's eyes lit up. "Yes, I would really like that. Can we make that happen?"

"Yes. Maybe this weekend?"

"You know I don't have plans. I don't have friends." Joseph laughed. He had read an article about this. Most men his age actually did not have friends, something called the epidemic of loneliness.

"Okay, I will call Rita and Bridgette and set it up." Ron said.

"Want to watch the game?" Ron said.

"Yea, I got some beers." Joseph went to the fridge.

Joseph walked past Ron's trophies and awards some of which still hung on the wall.

They sat down together and turned the game on.

"This guy sucks." Ron said.

"I wish they would just get rid of him." Joseph agreed as their least favorite player threw an interception.

"Remember when you caught that ball in your Williamsville game?" Joseph randomly asked Ron. Joseph loved to reminisce about his children's accomplishments.

"Yea, that was my longest catch of the year."

"That season was...interesting." said Joseph with a laugh.

"Good for me personally, but we sucked as a team."

"Yea, captain and second team tight end, but a 2-8 record....what are you gonna do?" Joseph asked.

"Yea, it was fun at times, but really wish we could have won some more." Ron said.

"Well, you guys never gave up at least, and you personally never gave up. That's how you earned 2nd team." Joseph said.

"A lot of good it did." Ron said sarcastically.

"Well, actually, I think it means a lot." Joseph said.

Ron frowned at him. "Not the Atticus Finch speech again."

"Seriously though" Joseph said. "Not everyone gets to have an undefeated season or go out on top. You just keep fighting no matter what."

Joseph knew his kids, and probably everyone else, tired of his philosophizing so he didn't pursue the topic with Ron. But Ron's example was perhaps a symbol. He did see Ron as an Atticus Finch type, or perhaps the protagonist from *The Old Man and the Sea*, someone who never really had a chance, but just keeps struggling anyway, knowing they are going to lose.

Ron had not been the best athlete but he worked hard against big odds, in the end his team wasn't successful, and Ron wasn't a superstar, but he got a little piece of the pie, he was named captain and made second team.

Maybe we are destined to lose, have been since the big bang, all the arbitrary arrangements come together and eventually break apart, like Vicky. But while these arbitrary arrangements are together, you milk them for all their worth. Maybe that was the only progress you could hope for.

"Finally!" Ron said excitedly as the quarterback threw a touchdown.

"He has pissed me off all season with his bullshit, but I have to admit, that was a beautiful pass." Joseph said.

"Yea." Ron held up his beer to his father and they clinked bottles.

Chapter 24
Year 2032

"Wow." Danielle said. "You were incredible." She laid back onto the bedsheets.

Joseph smiled. "You always say that. Be right back, I need to hit the bathroom."

Joseph collected his clothes and walked to the bathroom. He returned to find Danielle, wrapped in a sheet, squatting in front of his book case. She had a book out that Joseph had written.

"Um, were you ever going to tell me you are an author?" she said with false anger.

"Eventually. You knew I was a professor." He smirked.

"Yea, but I didn't know you were an author. That's cool. What do you write about?"

"Do you want the long boring version or the short version?" Joseph mocked himself.

"What, you think I can't understand it?"

"No! No!" Joseph protested. "Most people find what I write incredibly boring and or incomprehensible."

"Try me." She said.

"I have written a few books..."

"Wait, you have multiple books?"

"Look." He gestured to the book shelf.

She started to peruse the shelf.

"Wow."

"Don't be too impressed. No one reads this crap. I mean it. No one cares. In my profession, you need to write research articles. I don't like writing those, I love to write books because I feel like I have the freedom to say what I want. In a nutshell. I write about democracy, philosophical concepts, leadership and the arts,

"I doubt no one reads them." She shot him a look. The bedsheet clung tightly against her breasts. Her black hair hung and bounced around her cheeks as she scanned the books.

"Well, I have a couple of citations, but my editors said they wanted the sales a little higher though."

"It's still an amazing achievement."

"Who cares about this stuff," he picked her up, like a baby. She protested but he threw her on the bed and started kissing her.

At one point, he cared so much about these books, about his career, his citations, democracy. But, over time, that just faded. He never achieved the success he wanted or thought he deserved and maybe that soured his view. But he realized the only things that really mattered were his children, his wife, his loved ones, and now even Danielle. The only thing that really mattered were people and connections, whoever they may be with.

He began to kiss Danielle again.

Chapter 25
Year: 2032

"It's nice, to be all together." Joseph said as he took a sip of wine.

"Dad, I never see you drink." Rita said.

"I know, but this wine is good." He said.

"The oven beeped, I will take out the mac and cheese." Bridgette said.

"No, I will take it out." Rita said.

"No, I will." Bridgette snapped.

They both stomped into the kitchen.

"They are still fighting after 20 years?" Ron said to his father.

"It never stopped." Joseph said. "Pass the wine."

Both girls came to the table. Rita visibly annoyed at her sister.

"I see some things never change." Joseph said. "But you are adults now so you can do what you want." He took a swig.

"Anyway," Rita said, but she drew the word out and rolled her eyes and looked at her sister. Bridgette rolled her eyes in return.

They all dug into the mac and cheese.

"This is great." Ron said. "What's in there?"

"Bacon, relish and hamburger meat." Bridgette said.

"Pass the ketchup." Joseph pointed to the Ketchup bottle.

"What?" Rita said disgustedly.

"You heard me. Pass the ketchup. I like ketchup with hamburger mac and cheese."

Rita made a gagging face and passed the ketchup.

"This is such a good family recipe. When did we start eating this?" Bridgette asked the family. "Dad, did you make this up?"

"Your mom actually had the recipe. We just tweak it every time we make it." A silence fell over the family, until Ron changed the subject.

"So once a month? We are going to have dinner together?"

They all agreed.

"Okay, Let's hear it. I want to hear all the good things." Joseph said.

"How is the project going, that you were telling me about?" Joseph asked Ron.

"Good, its going really well. I think we are going to wrap it up soon."

"Were you the lead on that?" Rita asked.

"Yes, I had 40 people under me and mapped out the entire area."

"That is great."

"And of course, congrats are in order, for the master's degree." Joseph raised his glass toward Rita.

"Yes, I am so glad that is over!"

"Congrats." Ron said.

"Do you think you will pursue a doctorate?" Joseph asked.

"Let me enjoy the MA for a little while." Rita smiled.

"And your girls went undefeated, right?" "You guys won every game?" Ron asked Bridgette.

"Yes, we have two more games, and if we win those we get to the state championship. We also have the leading rebounder in the country."

"When you got to that high school, weren't they perennial losers?"

"Yea." Bridgette beamed.

All of you have done some amazing things. I am so proud." Joseph dabbed at his eye.

"Don't cry dad." Rita said.

"You know I love to hear about all your accomplishments"

"Yes Dad, we know. You ask us all the time." Bridgette grinned coyly.

"I am an old man and it makes me happy." Joseph smirked.

His kids could do things he could not, they were scholars and leaders and athletes, and they had surpassed him at every turn. This was evolution, this was progress.

"Do we have dessert?" Rita asked.

"Yes. I made it." Bridgette said.

"You made it?" Rita asked in a condescending manner.

"Yes, I can bake too Rita." Bridgette said defiantly.

"Can you two stop?" Ron said.

The girls sat across from each other. Joseph smiled. He had put up with their bickering for 20 years.

"What about you dad?" Rita asked.

"What about me?"

"Do you have something to tell us?" Rita gave him a mysterious grin. "I have to admit, It annoyed me a little at first, but I just don't want you to be alone." The other two nodded in agreement.

"Its just companionship," Joseph said, a little defensively.

"Dad, its okay." Bridgette said. She put her hand on his.

"I don't love her, like I loved your mother...its...companionship..." Joseph said again. "Also, understand, that all of my money and assets are in your name. She can't come in and take anything..."

"Dad, no one was worried about that." Ron said dismissively.

"I know you weren't because none of you are like that. But I just want you to know that all of my savings, the house, retirement, everything I have, which isn't much, is going to you guys when I die."

"Can we not talk about this?" Rita asked.

"Sorry, I just wanted you to know." Joseph said as he took a forkful of macaroni and cheese.

"We just want you to be happy." Bridgette said.

"I am. I mean, I always think of your mother, we knew each other for over 30 years, you cannot just sever a connection like that. When I think of her, I remember the past, or some shiny version of it, you know how nostalgic I get." All three children nodded in agreement.

"I think about college, how we met, how young she was, how vibrant, how athletic..." his voice trailed, then regained strength. "I remember the times before we had you, when we were just dating...she seemed like a different person before the disease. I really wish you could have known her then. One time, we went out to a club. She looked beautiful, I'll never forget she had on this tight green short dress with a little palm tree on it. No less than four guys asked her dance. Later, when she had you guys, she was so vibrant...I wish you could have seen her back then."

"I remember some of it," Ron said.

"Yes, she was incredible with you all, but especially you and Rita. Obviously, she loved you the same" Joseph gestured toward Bridgette "But by the time you were born," he paused "the sickness started taking a toll." While Joseph loved all his children the same, he always felt he had a special relationship with Bridgitte because Vicky had gotten sick and he had to tend to her more as a small child.

"I wish you could have known her..." he said while looking at a picture of her on the wall.

"We did know her Dad. She was an amazing person."

"I am going to the grave tomorrow." Joseph said.

"What time are you going?" Rita asked?

"Probably after lunch."

"So 11:01?" Rita joked. Joseph, for years, promptly ate his lunch at 11:00 am.

"Maybe a little later," he smiled. "Probably around 12:30."

"I can meet you there." Rita said.

"Me too." said Ron.

"I can't meet at that time, I will go later by myself." Bridgette said.

"What time are you done with practice?" Joseph asked her.

Around 6 ish." She said.

"I can meet you then." Joseph nodded.

"You are going to go twice?" Bridgette asked.

"Yea, that's fine. I want to see you."

"Okay, sounds good." Bridgette smiled.

"I wouldn't want to see her." Rita rolled her eyes.

"Stop-p-p-p..." Ron said.

"I'm kidding." Rita said. Bridgette ignored her.

All children were accidents in some sense, cosmic accidents which then somehow became invested with meaning and changed the course of history and the universe, temporary accidents becoming purposeful and meaningful, at least for a time.

Chapter 26
Year: 2032

He put his blinker on to exit the expressway and turned onto the back road that Danielle lived on. The snow storm had begun just like predicted. If it got too bad outside he might have to stay at her house. He had never stayed the night.

He slowed the car down as he approached her house. An old, but newly renovated, farmhouse stood in the middle of nowhere on a lonesome backroad, serene and perfect, isolated and beautiful. He needed to eat. There weren't too many food joints around but they could find something, or maybe they would cook. Whenever she called him, they usually discussed their plans but this time she just wanted him to come over. He turned the engine off, put his key fob in his pocket and walked to her front door through the wind.

When he entered her house, she sat on the couch and stared blankly at the cushion.

"I am so hungry." He said. "Can we eat? Is there anything open with the storm? Or do you have food here? If I were thinking, I would have brought some stuff..."

"Joe..." she said softly.

"Do you think the grocery store is open? I could make us hamburgers, or maybe some pulled pork, actually, that sounds amazing..."

"Joe." She said more sternly to get his attention.

"Yea?" he looked at her.

"I am getting back together with Scott."

"Wait, what?" Joseph said confused.

"I'm getting back together with Scott." Danielle said sheepishly again.

"Your ex?"

"Yea." She did not look at Joseph.

"Why?" he asked annoyed.

"It just makes sense. I mean, we were separated."

"You told me you were divorced when we first met." Joseph said sharply.

"I know, it was, is complicated." She frowned.

"Doesn't sound complicated." He said curtly.

"You and I were never officially together," she reminded him.

"I can see that." He said.

He did not love Danielle, at least not the way he loved Vicky, but it hurt, deep. Another connection severed.

"Why though? I don't understand. You said he was an asshole. He treated you like shit and didn't he cheat on you?"

Danielle still did not look at him.

"I know, but...we have a history together. I mean, we've been on and off since high school..."

"So, what was I? A distraction?" His voice began to rise. "I thought you said you don't usually have flings that weren't serious. I guess you broke your rule with me." He said sarcastically.

"You even said you didn't want to get married or anything." Danielle said defensively.

Yea, I didn't want to get married, but..." in Danielle's defense, they had never really solidified or defined their relationship. "I thought it was more than just a hook-up."

Danielle did not say anything.

"Whatever." He said.

He had a few things at her place and he began to collect them.

"It wasn't just a hook-up." She said as his back was turned. "I did have fun with you, I really did like you. But..." she paused. "I guess, sometimes we don't know why we do what we do."

He wanted to tell her about Schopenhauer's idea of the will, of raw instinct which animates us but is covered by reason and norms, the illusion of rationality. He decided against it.

"Yea, I guess so. Bye." He said flatly as he left her apartment.

"Wait," she said. "It's bad out there." She walked over to her window and opened the blinds. "Joe, I don't think you can go right now. The roads are a mess, especially around here they really do not plow. When I called you, I wasn't thinking about the storm, I didn't think it would be this bad…"

"Hmm…" he cut her off "maybe you should have thought of that before you told me you were fucking your ex."

"Stop it!" she began to cry.

"Maybe you could have told me that a little earlier. What do you want me to do? Sleep on the couch? Maybe we could have hot chocolate together and be friends and you tell me all about Scott and how big his dick is and how much money he has…"

"Please stop!" Tears came down her face and her mascara clotted into large clumps.

"You think I am some big slut! I'm not, I am...its...I am confused..." was all she could blurt out. "You don't know..." she trailed off with her head in her hands. She slumped into the seat cushion and curled up into a ball.

While he was not below taking shots at her, he did not think she was a bad person. Like she said, sometimes we don't know why we do the things we do. Connections form and are severed, they flicker, are hot and then die again, cold skeletons in cold space. Their connection flickered briefly and died for whatever reason.

"I'll take my chances." He said coldly.

She sniffled. "Please, stay at the motel in town. Or at least text me when you get home. Please."

"Doesn't Scott work for the town?" he asked the question he already knew the answer to. She looked at him with apprehension.

"Yes." She said meekly, unsure why he asked.

"Well then he can fucking scrape me off the road when the storm is over."

"Stop! Stop! Please text me, please..."

"Fuck you." He slammed the door on her crying face.

He sped. He did not usually speed. Too afraid of getting a speeding ticket but tonight he didn't care. The snow came down hard. Almost 10 inches to possibly a foot were expected by tomorrow morning. He did not care right now. He did not love Danielle like he loved Vicky, that was true. But the loss of that connection hurt.

Chapter 27
Year: 2032

After the car jackknifed with the bridge embankment, it came to a rather soft and gentle stop in the cushiony snow. Joseph hung upside down, but as far as he could tell, he was not confined or pinned. The steering wheel had dug hard into his side during the crash, and his ribs felt bruised, making it difficult for him to breathe. Each labored breath shot a radiating pain throughout his entire upper half and down to his torso.

Joseph worked through the pain and unbuckled his seat beat. He crawled out of the door and propped himself up onto the side of the car, near the rear passenger windshield. Surprisingly, the windshield had not cracked and he saw the matted upholstery of the rear passenger seat, complete with the little tear by the shoulder. This ugly upholstery, which still had a stain from when Bridgette spilled ketchup on it. He remembered one time his in-laws chastising him. *"Why did you never get that taken care of?"* His mother-in-law said. *"It looks terrible."* Joseph didn't really have answer for her at the time. He didn't know why he focused on that now, but there it was.

He continued his labored breath, each gasp of searing, all encompassing pain. But then he turned away from the upholstery and saw the field. The white field spread out like a picnic blanket. In the far distance the blanket was bordered by trees but only on the sides of the field. Overhead was a metallic grey sky at dusk. It almost seemed, *infinite*. The blank white and grey, the barrenness of the field and sky, overtook him in a way which made his senses obsolete and useless. The pain in his chest seemed little more than a papercut now. He laughed and cried but could not understand why.

Maybe, because for the first time in his life, he actually felt *free*. Maybe, the rat finally broke its cage. Sure, he couldn't really move, but physical freedom did not matter, he had something better now.

The infinite barrenness, the infinite white blank became the nothing before the something, the source of all creation and life in this random and forgotten field on the side of a deserted highway.

He thought of that smug priest, that fucking cocky bastard way back when. He thought of his grandfather. This nothingness, this blankness before human perception, before accidental intelligence, but in a paradoxical way, he needed his accidental intelligence to comprehend it, maybe his intelligence was a temporary appendage which he needed for a while, but no longer. Maybe the blank has always existed, waiting for him, ready to take him.

What the fuck was he doing? He needed to do something, make a call or crawl to that rest stop. But that rest stop was miles behind him. He touched his pocket that contained his phone only to realize the phone had been heavily damaged in the accident. He tried to make a call. Nothing. Panic began to set in. He might die out here. Jesus Christ, just like the fucking Jack London story, but instead of matches he had a broken cell phone. Like a postmodern Jack London.

He thought of his children. Thank God they were grown and he did not have to support them anymore. They were all more successful than him. He and Vicky had raised them right. They were successful, and more importantly, they were good people. And his book, he had just sent the final proofs to the editor. At least it would be published.

Something stuck in his leg. A lighter? These were the pants he wore when Vicky died in the hospital. The lighter must have gone through the wash, but maybe with some luck it would still work. Now seemed like a great time for a smoke. There wasn't much else he could do.

The cigar, which had been wrapped, lit up and the tiny flame gave him some momentary warmth. "It's a boy." He looked down and grinned at the print.

He thought of Ron. He smoked one of these at Ron's birth, over thirty years ago. He could barely inhale but the warm smoke filled his mouth and it felt good.

His children were *better than him* and nothing made him happier. This is how it should be, maybe this is evolution. Suddenly the passage that his uncle read at both his grandfather's and his grandmother's funeral popped into his head.

"I have fought the good fight, I have finished the race."

He repeated this to himself, as a sort of eulogy. The fight finally ended and like a weary boxer, he laid his head against the car.

He thought about trying to save himself (although there was not much he could do anyway), but a thought occurred to him. If he died, his children would inherit his holdings, albeit they were small, but still something.

His life insurance, equity, retirement and savings. They were all beneficiaries. Like *It's a Wonderful Life* or *Death of Salesman*. Joseph was no George Bailey, but perhaps he was a little bit like Willy Loman. Well, maybe a little better than Willy, but still a nobody. Danielle certainly would not miss him, but even now, he knew he did not love her.

Joseph did not have any real successes to call his own- except for his children. But they were not successes like bestselling books, no they were their own people. He puffed on the cigar through the pain and blew smoke into the infinite blank grey before him.

His children no longer needed him or Vicky, not anymore. He became discarded scaffolding or an orange peel, something important and integral for a time, but now, something no longer needed, redundant and unnecessary.

The blank grey canvass in front of him made him finally see. Maybe he witnessed the beginning of the world in the cold or the end of his accidental intelligence, the end of his arbitrary arrangement, shed like an orange peel. It served him well, but now he no longer needed it.

Night had fallen and his phone lay shattered, he had careened into a ditch and hour by hour more snow covered him relentlessly. No one would find him for days. No. He would die out here and accept it. Maybe Danielle's ex would actually find him, how poetic.

He could not fight anymore and he thought perhaps we win by *not* going back to the confines and we win by going *to* the barren white, to the infinite. That is true progress. We break the cage because we do not crawl back to the cholesterol medications, and celebrities and tech billionaires and insurance rates and political parties. We leave their supposed logic. We leave the accidental intelligences and arbitrary arrangements. We abandon all the temporary gods we erected to give us order (and then forgot we had built them) and we just succumb to the blank white.

Maybe, in one of those temporary iterations, the universe, and human beings, or whatever comes after us, may just figure it all out, but Joseph doubted that. This present iteration seemed like some sort of celestial joke.

But, if given the choice by some god, Joseph would have to pick this life, this celestial joke, this arbitrary configuration again, and again and again and again. In true Nietzschean fashion, Joseph would reaffirm this meaningless life by choosing it again, if only for his children.

And maybe progress lived here, in the snow, all along. The snow is lovely, dark and deep, and Joseph, this failed philosopher, had nonetheless kept all of his promises.

We go *toward* infinity. And then, we keep going further, we go to the end of infinity and keep going, maybe we make our own infinity beyond rules and logic and awards, beyond the binary positions we are appointed to. We build something of true permanence. We write a poem in the blank, and just keep writing until it makes sense.

The cigar puffed out, and Joseph threw the butt end in the snow. Maybe he could finally be useful, could be the living embodiment of a progress which eluded him his entire life.

But no, it would not be *his* progress. It would be his children's progress. Maybe the snow, the blank, the white, would also be the end of his progress and he would welcome the end.

He did not know who was correct, Hegel or Schopenhauer, but he really didn't care either. Here, in the cold, he, Joseph Joy, a number, one out of seven billion, would reject evolution, reject progress, reject this arbitrary arrangement and its gods, smoke a cigar and contentedly watch everyone else march into the future which he no longer wanted.

He had seen the stupidity, the cruelty and apathy, the suffering and mundanity in this configuration and did not think anyone could change it and he did not want to try anymore. Maybe his kids would figure it out, maybe his students, but he was tired.

There was only one thing left to do.

After he had died, the snow continued to fall, like it had for centuries before.

AUTHOR PROFILE

Angelo Letizia is a professor of education at Notre Dame College in Baltimore, Maryland. His true passion however is writing. He writes novels and poetry. Angelo's academic credentials include: PhD. in Educational Policy Planning and Leadership, *College of William and Mary;* MA. in European History, *Old Dominion University;* BA. in Secondary Social Studies, *State University of New York* at Cortland

www.ingramcontent.com/pod-product-compliance
Lightning Source LLC
Chambersburg PA
CBHW052139070526
44585CB00017B/1894